How to write
proposals
and reports
that get results

■   ■   ■

Myron L. Youngman
The Kaifa Group, Inc.
PO Box 288
Cedarville, OH 45314-0288

The Institute of Management (IM) is at the forefront of management development and best management practice. The Institute embraces all levels of management from students to chief executives. It provides a unique portfolio of services for all managers, enabling them to develop skills and achieve management excellence.

If you would like to hear more about the benefits of membership, please write to Department P, Institute of Management, Cottingham Road, Corby NN17 1TT.

This series is commissioned by the Institute of Management Foundation.

How to write proposals and reports *that get results*

■ ■ ■

ROS JAY

in the Institute of Management

FOUNDATION

PITMAN PUBLISHING

PITMAN PUBLISHING
128 Long Acre, London WC2E 9AN

A Division of Pearson Professional Limited

First published in this edition 1995

British Library Cataloguing in Publication Data
A CIP catalogue record for this book can be obtained
from the British Library.

ISBN 0 273 62202 1

10 9 8 7 6 5 4

Typeset by Northern Phototypesetting Co Ltd, Bolton
Printed and bound in Great Britain by Bell and Bain Ltd, Glasgow

The Publishers' policy is to use paper manufactured from sustainable forests.

About the author

ROS JAY is a business editor and a well known writer whose books include: *Build A Great Team!*, *Low Cost Marketing* and *Effective Presentation*.

Contents

■ ■ ■

Acknowledgements

■ ■ ■

The idea for this book grew out of a training guide I wrote for Video Arts Ltd to accompany their video Report Writing. I would like to thank Video Arts for their permission to incorporate some of that material into this book. The video Report Writing can be bought or hired by calling Video Arts on 0171-637 7288.

1
■ ■ ■

Introduction

How many reports or proposals are sitting in your in-tray at the moment? And in your out-tray? Every manager has to write reports or proposals occasionally – in fact for most of us it's a regular part of our job – reports to the board, monthly reports, research reports, proposals to customers. They are a standard management tool without which it would be impossible to function efficiently.

Despite this, most of us are never formally taught how to write them. It's just assumed that we'll know. And yet we've all read enough badly written reports to know that it isn't that simple. And the difference between a good and a bad report can be the difference between winning and losing a contract. A bad report may contain all the facts but presentation, in terms of structure and layout, is often the clinching factor.

Once you learn the skills of professional report and proposal writing – and like most skills they are easy once you know how – you are far more likely to get the results you want. You will instantly increase your chances of winning a major contract, convincing the bank manager to give you a loan, or persuading the board to accept your proposal for introducing flexitime.

Why do we need proposals and reports?
■ ■ ■

The purpose of proposals and reports is for the reader to understand something they didn't understand before and usually to persuade them to take a particular action. Some things are far more quickly explained verbally, but sometimes we need to record our facts and arguments on paper so they can be referred to later, or we want to distribute them to several people. Every time we do this we are writing a report of one kind or another. There are lots of kinds of report or proposal such as:

2

- interdepartmental memo
- monthly management report
- regular budget report
- report to internal committees
- proposal for a new company scheme
- new equipment request
- sales proposal.

Proposals and reports: the difference
■ ■ ■

This book deals with writing both proposals and reports because the skills are the same. However, there are some key differences in the aim of the two types of document:

Reports	Proposals
1 Contain information about what has happened in the past:	1 Examine what might happen in the future.

2 Seek primarily to inform the reader	2 Seek primarily to persuade the reader to make a particular decision.
3 Record objective facts.	3 Express opinions – albeit supported by objective facts.

What's in it for me?
■ ■ ■

It's a fair question. Why bother to improve our writing skills? Well, there are plenty of benefits for the reader and for your organisation. And there are plenty of advantages for *you*.

The reader

3

- A well produced report or proposal is easier to understand.
- It's quicker to read.
- It's more interesting – it tells you what *you* want to know.

The organisation

- A good report or proposal gives a better impression of the organisation.
- If it's a sales proposal, it will be more persuasive and so more likely to make a sale.
- If it's for internal use it will be more likely to generate the best decision.

You

- You will find it quicker, easier and more enjoyable to produce good reports once you know the skills.
- It will become a less stressful part of your job.
- You will be able to focus more clearly on the subject

while you're writing the document.

■ Your colleagues and bosses will be impressed.

■ Your credibility in the organisation will increase when your proposals and reports look professional and get results. Many management high fliers can date the start of their success from a particular report or proposal that was admired by people higher up the organisation.

■ You are more likely to be given the pick of the proposals and reports to write when yours have a reputation for being the best.

One other big advantage is that you'll find many of the skills you learn in this book are useful in other areas of management as well, such as planning presentations or exhibitions, market research, and writing job applications and business letters.

4

EXERCISE

Different people have different attitudes to writing reports and proposals. Read through the following statements and see how many of them apply to you.

'I quite enjoy writing them, but I worry what other people will think when they read them.' ☐

'I find reports and proposals difficult to write.' ☐

'I always find excuses not to get started.' ☐

'I dread having to write a report.' ☐

'I always have this sneaking feeling that I'm writing complete nonsense.' ☐

'I'm good at persuading people face-to-face, but I don't seem to be able to do it on paper.' ☐

'I never know how to start.' ☐

'I never know when to stop.' ☐

'I'm not sure how much supporting information to include,

so I usually put it all in to be on the safe side.' ☐

'It always seems to take me ages to write a report or
proposal.' ☐

'I can spend hours trying to think of the right word.' ☐

'I hate writing reports.' ☐

All of these attitudes are common and quite understandable.
We're never at our best when we're not sure what we're
doing. Remember learning to drive? Do you remember being
terrified to accelerate up to 20 miles an hour? And being
incapable of holding a conversation when the engine was
running, even if the car was stationary? It took me ages to
get the hang of steering – I couldn't see how experienced
drivers could get into cars and just steer them. It didn't
seem possible.

5

Now, of course, we're happy to listen to the radio while we
cruise down the motorway at 70 mph. And once you've read
this book and learnt the skills it explains, you'll be breezing
through reports and proposals in the same way.

2
■ ■ ■

The objective

The more thinking you do at the start of the process of writing a proposal or report, the less work you will have to do later. The first thing to think about is what you want the report to achieve.

You need to start by setting a clear objective – a single sentence outlining the aim of the proposal or report. The more specific you can make your objective before you start to write, the more easily you will be able to focus once you begin writing. This focus is vital for several reasons:

- It makes it easier to see what information should be included.
- It makes it easier to see what information should be omitted.
- It helps you to remain consistent throughout the report, in content and style.

This chapter looks at the reasons for setting a clear objective, how to do it and how to make the objective specific.

Why set an objective?
■ ■ ■

What we want to do is to put our objective down on paper in a single sentence. We'll look at exactly how to do this in a moment. But first of all let's consider *why* we want to do it. A clear, written objective has a number of benefits:

1 It helps to pitch the report in the most suitable way for the people who will be reading it.

2 It helps you to keep a clear focus.

3 It gives the final report or proposal more clarity if someone else incorporates it into a broader report.

4 It makes it easier to research.

5 It makes it easier to write.

6 It makes it easier to read.

Pitching the proposal or report

It's important to think about the kind of person or people who will be reading the proposal, and make sure it's written in the best way for them. The idea is to compile a profile of the readers, because it makes a difference to the content and style of what you're going to write.

EXERCISE

Imagine you are trying to persuade your family to go on a camping holiday for the first time.

1 Think of three or four main points you would want to bring out if you were discussing it with your partner.

2 Now think of the main points you would want to make if you were trying to convince the kids.

RESPONSE

If you were talking to your partner, you'd probably bring out points such as:

- How much cheaper it would be than staying in an hotel.

- How much less it would matter if the kids were embarrassing/noisy/dirty.

- How comfortable modern tents can be.

- That you can always eat out if no-one feels like cooking.

- That there'll be more to occupy the kids in the evenings so they'll be less grouchy.

- That the kids will be so exhausted by the end of the day they'll be asleep by 8 o'clock.

9

To convince the kids you'd be emphasising:

- How much less you'll have to nag them about being embarrassing/noisy/dirty.

- That they can play at being explorers.

- That you'll teach them to make a camp fire and cook sausages on it.

- That they can go to bed later than usual.

This exercise illustrates the reason you need to understand who your readers are before you start work on your report. A clear objective helps you to pitch the report appropriately for the type of reader it is aimed at. Otherwise you could waste a lot of time telling them something that they aren't interested in, or that they already know – or you could lose them completely by failing to explain something that they *don't* know about. You could even emphasise a point which you see as a benefit without realising that they regard it as a drawback.

Your proposal may be intended for only two or three readers, but they may have very different outlooks on the subject. For example, a sales proposal may be read by your client company's MD, Chief Accountant and Production Manager. Obviously they will all have different priorities. However, as long as you've thought about this, you can make sure that you emphasise the most important points for each of them, without wasting too much time on aspects which are of no concern to any of the three.

Keeping a clear focus

10

Once you have a clear objective, it helps you to focus on what you are doing. You'll find it far easier to decide how much time to spend on a certain point, whether to explain the technical details which support a point, or whether to include a particular graph in the main body of the report rather than in the appendix.

You'd have thought it would be possible to make these decisions without sitting down and writing out an objective first – especially if you know your readers well and have written reports for them before. Well yes, it is possible. But it's still better to start with an objective, for two reasons:

1 It's all too easy to become so used to writing for certain people that we don't really think about it any more. And a lot of the time we get away with it – which is why we do it. But every so often we fail to notice that something has changed. Perhaps this time the MD, who normally supports ideas from your department, is resistant. Maybe your department looks as if it may overspend its budget this year, so new spending will be looked on less favourably than usual. Or perhaps the customer you are

writing the proposal for is less well inclined towards you after the mess up over last month's delivery.

2 Even if things really haven't changed, you'll still be able to focus better with a clear objective to help you. You might get there in the end without it, but an objective provides a short cut, with less scope for making mistakes – and why do something the long way round when you don't need to?

Preserving clarity if the report is incorporated into a broader proposal

Quite often someone will ask for a report from more than one person and will then combine these, often adding more information themselves, into one large proposal or report. For example, your company may produce a proposal to a customer for supplying and maintaining a fleet of lorries. You may only be asked to write the maintenance section. If your contribution is in any way confused when you submit it, it will be far more so by the time the sales manager has incorporated it into the larger document.

What's more, this larger submission, or parts of it, may even be used in the same way to create yet another proposal – and why not? If the information already exists on paper it's far more efficient to use that original report than to start again. The customer may use it as part of a proposal to *their* board, to persuade them to run their own fleet of vehicles. But if your material was unclear at the start, it will be harder still to follow once it reaches this stage.

Again, the objective will ensure that your report or proposal is sufficiently clearly focused to remain clear even if it is put into a different context.

It's easier to research

One of the mistakes a lot of people make when they set about producing reports is to research all the information they can

11

get their hands on and then work it all into the report. This makes for very long-winded reports indeed. It's usually the case that most of the information, while relevant to the subject in general, is not relevant to the particular scope of the report. Not only does this make the report heavier to read, it also takes far longer to research.

If, however, you have set a clear objective before starting, you can use it as a touchstone against which to test each possible area of research, and see whether or not you need to pursue it.

It's easier to write

If you aren't clear in your mind before you start to write, it's far easier to miss things out or decide halfway through that you should have put the emphasis on a different aspect of the subject. A proper objective will save you time and make it easier for you to write the report because the structure and content will flow far more smoothly.

It's easier to read

You must have tried to read other people's material which is hard to follow and badly structured. That's because they didn't really know what they were doing when they started. If you're clear about what you're trying to achieve and the key topics you want to tackle, this will come across to the readers. Not only will they find the proposal or report easier to read, they will also be more convinced of your grasp of the subject.

Setting the objective
■ ■ ■

You need to be clear in your own mind exactly what the proposal or report is trying to achieve. You probably have a broad idea before you start to write the objective; your aim will be 'to convince the customer to buy one of our swimming pools' or 'to review the performance of the main switchboard'. But now you need to tighten the focus, and be more specific.

The first step is to think about the people you're writing the report or proposal for, and look at the subject from their viewpoint. In order to do this you need to ask yourself various questions:

- Who is the proposal for?
- What is their level of knowledge of the subject?
- What will they use the proposal for?
- What aspects do they particularly want covered?
- What does the proposal *not* need to cover?

As we saw earlier, this should help you decide how to pitch the report. If you're writing a sales proposal for a very wealthy client with money to spare you won't want to waste too much time justifying the price of your swimming pools. If you're writing a report for your MD on the problems with your main switchboard you probably won't want to dwell on the technical minutiae. So the precise nature of the objective will be affected by who is going to read the report.

13

Making the objective specific

Imagine you're in Watford, and you want to go to New York. You could strike out in a vaguely Westerly direction and start asking the way somewhere around Cardiff. Eventually you might find a boat headed towards the US and when you arrived you could start hitching to New York. There's a fair chance you'd get there in the end – after a fashion.

But that isn't what most of us do. We establish the most efficient way to get there before we start; a way that doesn't only get us to New York but does it comfortably, quickly, economically and in accordance with any other requirements we have.

This is also by far the best way to write proposals and reports. We need to work out in advance not only where we are going, but also what the main requirements of the route are, and what aspects of the subject we particularly want to visit on the way.

To convince the customer to buy one of our swimming pools

To demonstrate that our deluxe swimming pool meets the customer's needs.

To demonstrate that our deluxe swimming pool meets the customer's needs, especially in terms of quality and ease of maintenance.

14

Let's have a look at one of the earlier examples. The general aim was 'to convince the customer to buy one of our swimming pools'. But that could apply to lots of customers with very different requirements. So how can you make this objective more specific? You could say 'to demonstrate that our deluxe swimming pool meets the customer's needs'. That's more specific but it still doesn't tell you *which* needs. How about 'to demonstrate that our deluxe swimming pool meets the customer's needs, especially in terms of quality and ease of maintenance'?

That will make it far easier to focus when you're writing the report, and will be more useful as a guideline for measuring information against to see whether it should be included in the proposal.

15

EXERCISE

Here are three more broad objectives for reports or proposals; try to make them more specific. For the purpose of the exercise you can supply your own conditions to narrow the scope. You can aim the report at anyone you think appropriate, as long as you decide clearly who it is.

1 To review the performance of the main switchboard.

2 To recommend extending the product range to include an extra large size for all the major product lines.

3 To persuade a customer to take out a computer maintenance contract with your company.

RESPONSE

There is no single answer to any of these, and it makes a great deal of difference who you decided you were writing the report for. But here are some ideas on each objective.

1 To review the performance of the main switchboard.

- Whom is the report aimed at? Your MD? The company that supplied the switchboard? Your technical manager?

- Are you examining whether to improve its performance, how to improve it, or whether to get rid of the thing and invest in a better switchboard?

- Are you looking at its performance in terms of cost, efficiency or breakdowns?

2 To recommend extending the product range to include an extra large size for all the major product lines.

- Who are you writing for? The production department? The board?
  The bank? Your distributors?

- Are you looking at the likely success of the extended range? The cost of introducing it? The technical problems involved in production?

3 To persuade a customer to take out a computer maintenance contract with your company.

- Have they already got a maintenance contract with someone else,
  or none at all? Did they buy their computer system from you?

- Do they need to be persuaded of the value of a maintenance contract in general, or do you just have to convince them that yours is the best?

- How important to them are the various factors – price, speed of response, backup support etc.?

If you're used to giving presentations, organising exhibition stands, advertising and a host of other business skills, you'll recognise the need to start with a clear, specific objective. If not, you'll find that this is an invaluable technique for any project – not only for writing proposals and reports.

Write the right proposal
■   ■   ■

There's one more incredibly useful function that a properly thought out objective serves. Most of us have fallen foul of this problem at some time: suppose, as often happens, someone else has asked you to write a report – perhaps your boss. Maybe they've asked you to write a report on the exhibition at which you took a stand last week.

So off you go, and put a great deal of time and effort into producing a report. When you hand it to them, confidently expecting a pat on the back for all your hard work, they say 'No, no, no. This isn't what I wanted at all.' Apparently they didn't want a report on the company's performance, number of contacts, sales and so on at all. They wanted to know how well organised and advertised the exhibition was as a whole, how many people visited the show, what their profile was and so on.

17

I have heard people argue for hours over whose fault this is. It really doesn't matter. What matters is preventing it from happening again – and a well designed objective will do just that.

1 Make your objective specific. For example: 'To review the company's performance at last week's exhibition in terms of the response from customers and prospects.'

2 Write this down and show it to your boss, or whoever asked for the report.

3 At this stage they can say: 'No; I meant I wanted you to look at the overall exhibition – I know our results weren't

brilliant and I want to find out how much of that was due to the show being badly organised and how much was down to us.'

4 Because you showed the objective to your boss before starting work, you've only wasted five minutes instead of five days. Go away and come up with a fresh objective, and show it to your boss again to make sure you're on the right track this time.

Always go through this procedure when someone else has asked you to produce a proposal or report – even if you think you know what's wanted. The rest of this book is about writing the report correctly, but it's all wasted if you're not writing the correct report.

18

Summary

1 The first thing you need to do when you write a report or proposal is to work out the objective.

2 Ask yourself who you are writing the report or proposal for.

3 Think about what these readers will want to know and what their level of knowledge is.

4 Now make the objective as specific as you can and write it down – preferably in one sentence.

5 If you have been asked to write the report by someone else, show them the objective before you start work, to make sure there are no misunderstandings about its precise subject and emphasis.

19

3

■ ■ ■

Collecting the information

So what are you going to say in your proposal or report? Once you've set your objective you'll have a much clearer idea, but you won't know every last point, each precise argument, all the supporting facts. You'll have to go and research them.

When you've found all the information you'll probably end up with a pile of papers, books, magazine cuttings, reports, statistics, notes, brochures and other bits and pieces on your desk. This is the part a lot of people hate most. Where on earth do you start? How do you get from 18 inches of precariously balanced data to a few neat pages of typescript?

Well, before you ever lift a pen (or turn on a word processor) you need to organise the information you have. It needs to be collated into sections; once you've done that the task will look far easier because you only have to deal with one modestly-sized section at a time.

This chapter looks at these two stages of preparation which happen before you start to write:

1 Research.
2 Organise.

Research
■ ■ ■

What information do you need?

This is clearly the first question you will have to answer. The best thing to do at this point is to have a thinking session. You could do this on your own or with other people – whichever you find is most helpful for the proposal or report you're writing. Just jot down all the key areas you think you need to cover. And the objective you have written should help you.

Suppose your objective was:

'To review the current attractions in our theme park, and propose three new attractions which add variety for the customer, without exceeding a total budget of £75 0000.'

If you are writing this for the board of directors, you'll know what their current level of knowledge is, and where their interests lie. Let's imagine (not unreasonably) that finance is their main concern. How much will it cost and how much revenue will it generate? This should already give you a pretty clear idea of what areas to cover:

1 Brief round-up of the current attractions.

2 List of possible additions.

3 Costings for each option.

4 Technical details for each option.

5 Anticipated revenue for each option.

6 Recommendation.

The first part of your thinking session should involve jotting down each of these areas as a heading. These aren't the headings you will use in the final proposal – they're just to help you think clearly – so it doesn't matter what order you put them in. Under each of these headings you can then list the chief topics to include. For example, under section one, the round-up of current attractions, you would probably need to include:

- list of attractions (including brief description)
- running costs of each attraction (power consumption, number of staff required, food and keep for animals and so on)
- number of visitors to each attraction (including any seasonal fluctuations)
- price of each attraction (and turnround time between visitors or groups of visitors)
- overall income of each attraction (gross and net).

23

EXERCISE

Now it's your turn. Thinking logically, draw up a list of the main areas to cover under each of the following headings for the theme park attractions:

1 List of possible additions (just the areas to cover – not the actual attractions).

2 Costings for each option.

RESPONSE

There isn't a definitive list, of course, but here is an idea of the topics you could have included under each heading.

1 List of possible additions:

- description of attractions which could fit into a theme park

- amount of space each one would occupy (and any other conditions, eg must be near water)

- why each one would add variety

- how each one would fit into the current range (for marketing purposes)

- details of where else each one is used (other theme parks, where the nearest one to this site is, popularity at other sites and so on).

2 Costings for each option:

- basic cost of materials and stock

- building costs

- maintenance and running costs (power consumption, food and keep for animals and so on)

- staff costs

24

As you can see, by the time you've been through all the headings you have effectively drawn up a series of lists of the information you need to include in your proposal. Of course, for some proposals and reports you'll need to go through this process before you have any idea of where to begin, while for others you'll know most of it before you start. But it's still a vital stage because if you miss anything out now, you won't get another opportunity to remember it.

Don't cut corners

If you are confident you know what you're doing – it's only an internal memo or a routine management report – you may well be right. Even so you should at least look at the objective and work out in your mind the main headings. The fact is that it's the jobs we've done a hundred times before that we're most likely to get wrong. We don't question or double-check ourselves. We just assume we're doing it right, so we're far less likely to notice if one factor has changed.

If you've been writing a monthly management report for 18 months in your present job, you probably always have the same headings which you use as prompts to remind you what areas to write about. But you may be missing headings because certain areas haven't arisen before. For example, maybe one of your team has just handed in their notice. If it's the first time since you took over the job that anyone's left, you may never have included a section into which it fits and you could easily forget to mention it altogether. So always give your mind a chance to look beyond the usual boundaries, just to make sure there's nothing new which needs to be included in the report.

Where will you get the information from?

25

Once you've got your basic list written, you can go through and decide how best you can make the points you want to emphasise in each area. For example, you may decide that the best way to demonstrate the popularity of potential future attractions would be to get hold of research data from other theme parks which already use them. When it comes to working out the maintenance and running costs, perhaps the monthly management figures give you enough information about your current attractions to be able to calculate them. You can find out the cost of materials and stock from suppliers and get quotes from builders, and so on.

There are all sorts of places you can go for information, once you've decided what you want to know. In the case of the theme park attractions, for example:

Written information

- *books and booklets:* perhaps studies of the psychology of visitors – do they prefer adventure, fear or cuddly animals?

- *catalogues, brochures, leaflets and so on:* from your own park and from others

- *newspapers and magazines, including the trade press:* articles about theme park attendances, latest trends and so on

- *statistics:* from the press, trade associations and so on: about attendance levels, seasonal fluctuations, prices different parks charge etc.

- *regular management reports and monthly figures:* costs and popularity of your current attractions

- *other people's reports and proposals:* ideas put forward in the past, technical and financial data

- *notes you've taken at meetings or seminars:* how to encourage visitors, perhaps, or the disruption entailed in building a new attraction.

26

Public information

- *libraries – for directories of businesses, associations, local authorities, market research reports, newspapers and magazines:* any relevant research concerning the leisure industry, details of other non-competing parks to whom you could talk

- *trade associations and regulatory bodies:* useful information such as surveys into what people look for in a theme park, other theme parks' annual reports etc.

- *government departments – the Central Statistical Office lists government publications. You can also get information from other departments and quangos, from the DTI to the Inland Revenue:* for example you could consult the Health and Safety Executive for advice and recommendations on installing a centrifuge or a water ride.

Talking to people

- *interviews (take notes) – on the telephone or face-to-face:*

you could survey customers to find out what other kinds of activities they would like, or ask non-competing theme parks about their experiences.

■ *talking to the experts in the field – within the organisation and outside it:* who is best informed about the latest trends in theme park attractions? And you could talk to your internal technical people about their views on the suggested future attractions from a technical viewpoint

■ *asking suppliers for information and quotes:* builders, equipment suppliers and so on.

It's worth mentioning copyright briefly. If you use anybody else's material without their permission – such as sections of annual reports, published statistics and so on – you may be in breach of copyright. Yes, even if you only circulate the material to five members of the board and it never leaves the building. You have three options:

1 There is no copyright on ideas, only on words. So if you use the gist of the material, but rewrite it in your own words, you are within the law.

2 You can contact the holder of the copyright, who may be happy to let you use their material for nothing, or may charge you a fee.

3 If you don't know who owns the copyright, or want advice, contact the British Copyright Council (on 0171-580 5544).

What arguments will you put forward?

You now know what information you are planning to impart in your proposal, but what is it there for? It's there to explain or add weight to your case – that a centrifuge would be better than a Ninja Turtles water ride, or that your swimming pools are easier to maintain than your competitors'.

27

So the final part of your research must involve writing down the key arguments. These aren't facts that you have researched, these are opinions – although you will need to back them up with hard facts and figures.

If you are a sales person you will know the difference between features and benefits. Take any product or service – a feature is what it does, but a benefit is what it does *for the customer*. So a feature of a coat might be that it's made of thick wool, the benefit is that it keeps you warm.

At this stage in your research you probably have a desk full of information about features. What you need to do now is to go through your original list of headings again and make notes of all the benefits you want to emphasise. For example, when it comes to discussing staff costs for the possible attractions you could include in your theme park, you'll want to draw attention to the fact that the centrifuge only needs one person to operate it and it only takes a day to train them – whereas the Ninja Turtle water ride (you'll want to point out) requires four full-time personnel, two of whom will need extensive training.

Organise

■ ■ ■

Collate

So now you've collected together all the information you need to write your report or proposal. You're surrounded by piles of books and scraps of paper and are ready to start putting the material into some kind of order.

The first thing to do is to work through all the information you've collected and write down each main point on a separate piece of paper. This may sound long-winded, but it will save you a great deal of time later on, as well as helping you to think more clearly and methodically. If you have made your notes on a word processor, of course, all you'll have to do is

28

print them out and cut up the paper leaving one point printed on each piece.

This doesn't actually take very long. It isn't necessary to write down all the details – just the point they support. So your piece of paper might say on it: 'table comparing popularity and price of attractions'. You don't have to write out the whole table (although you'll find it useful to make a note of where to find the information later).

I usually find that if I'm only taking one or two pieces of information from a single source I write them out in full – then I've finished with the source book, magazine or whatever it was and my desk starts to look a bit clearer. When I've finished this part of the process I have a lot of pieces of paper and just three or four books, documents or whatever. Everything useful in these three or four sources still has its own corresponding bit of paper, but these particular pieces of paper contain only notes and references rather than the full data.

29

The chances are that if you were feeling overawed by the prospect of producing this proposal or report before, you'll start to feel happier at this point. For one thing, you now have very little on your desk apart from a lot of little pieces of paper, a situation which has a far more manageable feel to it than all those piles of books, articles and documents. And for another thing, there is no need to remember anything any more. It's all there, on those little scraps of paper. You can go away for a whole weekend and forget all about it, and when you come back on Monday morning, all the things you wanted to say will be waiting on your desk for you.

Sort into groups

The final stage of preparation is to sort all the information you have into logical groups. These may well be the headings you worked out at the start – when you were still in the process of deciding what you needed to know. To be honest, it doesn't matter much what groupings you use, as long as they make logical sense. This is not the structure you will finally use for the report or proposal, because you aren't arranging the groups into any order. But you need to go through this stage for three reasons:

1 It's an invaluable mental exercise; it helps you to organise your mind and focus clearly on the subject of the report or proposal.

2 As you work through the pieces of paper, allocating each one to the most logical group, you have a chance to check each one against the original objective for the report. This way you can make sure that you don't include any repeated points, or points that are unnecessary because the readers already know them, or aren't concerned with that aspect of the subject.

3 You will probably incorporate most of these groups into your eventual structure for the report or proposal, so this exercise is a useful preparation for that stage (which we'll deal with in the next chapter).

EXERCISE

Here's a chance to practise organising points into logical groups.

1 Imagine you're moving house and the place you're moving to needs a lot of work. How many different – but logical – ways could you organise your list of 'work to do'?

2 Suppose you wanted to explain the structure of your organisation to someone. Before you go into the nitty-gritty details, you'll want to

give them an overview. How many different ways can you think of to organise it into related groups?

RESPONSE

1 Here are four different ways you could organise the list of work:

- Room by room.

- According to the type of job – electrical, plumbing, decorating and so on.

- By importance – major structural work, minor structural repairs, cosmetic work.

- According to cost – jobs which will cost more than £1000, jobs costing between £200–£500, jobs between £50 and £200 and work costing less than £50.

2 You could explain the structure of an organisation in several ways, for example:

- By department – so your 'groups' would be accounts, production, sales, admin. and marketing, for example, before you start detailing how many people work in each, what their functions are and so on.

- By location – head office in Birmingham; two sections in Wales, one in Cardiff and one in Aberystwyth; three in Scotland and the north
  . . . and so on.

- Chronologically – the business started as a production company, selling to wholesalers. Then it developed its own sales team and later added a marketing department. Then it bought up three smaller breweries . . . etc.

You may have been wondering how long all this is supposed to take. There's no exact answer to that, but it depends on how important the final document will be. If there's a chance that the proposal could win you a million pound contract if it's good enough, it's probably worth putting a lot of effort into it. On the other hand it won't be worth spending two days preparing a memo asking your team to submit their expenses on the 25th of the month instead of the 26th in future.

You need to calculate the cost of your time against the possible revenue from the report or proposal. And don't forget to consider the personal benefits – if this document is likely to be seen by influential people higher up the organisation, who you want to notice you, you may feel it's worth spending extra time on it.

32

Once you've sorted your pieces of paper into groups you've finished collecting and collating your information, and it's time to think out the structure of the report or proposal. Now that you've prepared thoroughly, you've made the next stage much easier for yourself .

Summary

Research

1 Start by deciding what information you need. Using the objective as your reference, list the areas you need to cover.

2 For each of these general areas create a list of specific topics to research.

3 Go and find the information you need – use written sources, publicly available information, and talk to people.

4 Add your own notes of any benefits you want to emphasise.

Organise

1 Copy each point (or a note of it) onto a separate piece of paper. | 33 |

2 Sort these pieces of paper into logical groups.

4
■ ■ ■

Structure I: Proposals

Jean-Luc Godard once said that a film should have a beginning, a middle and an end 'but not necessarily in that order'. A *good proposal* is less flexible – they should definitely be in that order. Like a story, a proposal should keep its readers' attention and lead them smoothly from one point to the next. This is far easier to write and it's easier to read as well.

Readability is terribly important. Sometimes the people you write your proposal for are really keen to see it, but quite often you have far more of a vested interest in their reading it than they do themselves. Maybe you've come up with an idea that you feel is really promising, but the boss has said 'Well, I'm not sure. If you put your proposal in writing I might consider it.' Or a customer just wants to buy the best product they can get; they don't care whether it's yours or your competitor's – but you do.

The more readable, interesting and well-written your proposal is, the more likely these people are to read it. And the better disposed towards you they will feel. And structure is crucial to the coherence and smooth flow of a proposal.

All proposals which are designed to persuade, convince or sell, should follow the same format. (The next chapter will look at how to structure a report which simply provides information.) This means you can present your argument clearly and logically – as if you were writing a story.

The structure
■ ■ ■

As I mentioned before, the structure is very simple: beginning, middle and end. You could call it setting the scene, developing the story, resolving the story – a kind of business version of boy meets girl, boy loses girl, boy finds girl.

There are lots of different ways of expressing the idea, but they all mean the same thing. One of the easiest ways to remember it is the three 'P's:

- **Position:** where we are now.
- **Problem:** why we can't stay there.
- **Proposal:** where we should go to instead.

The process is very simple to follow. You start by explaining what the present situation is; then you look at the problem – why things need to change. Finally you make a recommendation as to the best solution to the problem. Very often you find that the final, 'proposal', section can be split into two sections: a round-up of the options followed by a recommendation as to which one to adopt. If you consider this as two distinct sections, you can think of the structure as having four parts, instead of three:

- **Position**
- **Problem**
- **Possibilities**
- **Proposal**

One reason that this structure is so easy to follow is because we have all grown up listening to stories which follow this format. Take Hansel and Gretel as an example:

Position

Hansel and Gretel were left in the wood by their parents, who couldn't afford to look after them any longer.

Problem

They found a house made of gingerbread, but unfortunately it belonged to a wicked witch who imprisoned them.

Possibilities

They could try to escape or they could trick the witch. Otherwise, they would be cooked and eaten by her.

Proposal

In the end the best option was to trick the witch by pushing her into her own oven so she burnt to death and then running away. And Hansel and Gretel escaped and ran home.

37

Here's another (less gruesome) example; this time a business fairy story. I've written it in simplistic language, not because I want to insult your intelligence, but in order to demonstrate how similar a proposal is to a fairy story (at least in structure).

Position

Once upon a time there was a nice, kind business that gave lots of people jobs.

Problem

As the years went by, things changed in the world. But the business didn't notice for a long time. After a while, the people who worked there stopped saying 'I'm so lucky to work for such a kind business'; instead they started to grumble. They began to say 'Other businesses are nicer to work for these days. My neighbour doesn't have to go to work until ten o'clock in the morning, so he can take his children to school first. Why can't our business be like that?'

Eventually, news of the people's complaints reached the ears of the Directors. At first they said 'Nonsense. This is a kind, friendly business; of course we're being as nice to our workers as we can. These are just the grumblings of a few troublemongers.' But after a while they began to realise that it wasn't just a handful of people who were complaining, it was almost everyone. At last they said "Perhaps we should at least think about this. We might be able to be even kinder to our people than we already are.' So they decided to see what they could do.

Possibilities

They thought about what would happen if they left things as they were. They thought about what would happen if they let people start work any time up to ten o'clock and then work for eight hours. And they thought about letting people come and go as they pleased until they had worked 35 hours in a week.

Proposal

At last they went back to the people and said: 'We pride ourselves on being a kind business, so we're doing what we can. These are the three ideas we've thought of.' Then they explained the three ideas and how they would work. At the end, they said 'We don't want to leave things as they are, because we don't like you being unhappy. And we think the third idea is too complicated, at least at the moment. So we suggest the middle idea. You can all start work any time between eight and ten o'clock, and stay for eight hours. That means you could be finished by four o'clock if you wanted to, or you could have a bit of extra time at home in the mornings.'

So that's the four 'P's. You might not use these words as section headings for your proposal (although you might), but that is effectively what the sections will be. Now let's have a look at each of the four stages in a bit more detail.

Position

■ ■ ■

Explaining the current position might appear to be stating the obvious. But in fact, it may not be as obvious as you think. For example, how would you describe British Rail before privatisation? It rather depends on your political views. You might describe it as anything from a shambles which could only be run properly by private commercial interests, to a stalwart public service which is sinfully underfunded. It would be extremely hard to be totally objective. But whatever your view, your readers need to know.

If you were a member of the Transport and General Workers Union writing for your union leaders, you would write from a very different angle to the one you would take as a Tory MP at the Department of Transport. But if you were a senior manager at British Rail your readers wouldn't know where you were coming from and would need you to tell them so they could see whether you were all on the same track.

So you need to make sure that you and your readers are all starting from the same position. But that's not the only reason for summarising the position at the start of your proposal:

- It helps people to focus on the right part of the issue. If you've written a proposal for your Board of Directors, some of the non-executive members of the board might know that your proposal is something to do with needing more company cars, but they may not have realised that it was specifically about the need for the PR department to have cars.

- It shows that you understand the background. The readers are far more likely to accept your proposed solution if they can see that you understand the problem.

- It gives you a chance to inform those readers who don't know without patronising those who do. The tone is not

'I'm telling you this because you don't know it'; it's 'Let's just make sure we're all agreed exactly what we're talking about.' Nevertheless, this gives you an opportunity to explain the position to any readers who are ignorant of it.

- It ensures that every reader has taken on board all the facts necessary to follow the rest of the proposal or report. It's like checking that everyone embarking on a trekking holiday together has all the essential equipment in their rucksacks before you set off on the first leg of the journey.

Content

You may find that you can state the position in a single sentence, or it may take a while to explain – you identified your readers' level of knowledge when you worked out your objective. Obviously if it's relatively low you may need to explain quite a lot. You may also have to run through a bit of history to explain how the present position was reached – that's fine, if it helps the reader.

Stating the position also gives you a chance to prove that you understand things from the reader's point of view. This is especially valuable if you're writing a sales proposal. Suppose your company sells photocopiers. Your proposal to a potential customer should not start by telling them *your* position – that your company 'started out selling printing blocks back in 1657 and now markets a range of photocopiers . . .'. The idea is to state the *reader's* position. So you start by saying that they 'have a photocopier which they've leased for the last 12 years . . .' and so on. Of course your position might be the same as the reader's – or it might not – that's irrelevant. Their position is the one that matters.

EXERCISE

Summarise briefly how you might state the position from the reader's point of view for each of the following proposals:

1 A proposal to a retail outlet to persuade them to stock your new range of citrus fruit squeezers.

2 A proposal to the marketing director at head office to launch an advertising campaign in your region.

3 A proposal to a business customer to use your vegetarian pizza delivery service for their business lunches.

RESPONSES

1 Orange and lemon squeezers always sell well, especially in the summer. Last year you sold as many as 20 a week during the hottest part of the summer.

2 Sales in the North East have been lower than in most other areas for the past two years. Evidence suggests that public awareness of our products is lower than elsewhere, possibly because our product has more local competition here than in the rest of the country.

3 You quite often invite business visitors to lunch; because you have no kitchen facilities you buy in food from outside. Someone normally goes out for sandwiches from the local shop; they get a selection because you don't usually know what your visitors' tastes are.

Problem
■ ■ ■

The function of this section of the proposal is to establish why you need to do anything at all – why the present position can't continue. This could be something bad, but it doesn't have to be. It could be an opportunity that you mustn't miss. For example:

Bad

- demand is changing
- equipment is wearing out
- staff are leaving
- money is being wasted
- there is new competition in the market
- offices are becoming overcrowded.

Good

- there is scope for a new product
- a small investment in new equipment could increase profit margins
- there's a new and much cheaper source of raw materials
- a perfect site has come up on the new trading estate
- trade barriers to Europe are coming down
- new legislation means things that were impossible before are now possible.

This is the section of the proposal most likely to meet with resistance from the reader, so it's especially important to validate your statement of the problem with hard evidence – we'll look at this more closely in Chapter 6.

The idea is that by the time you've finished explaining the problem, the reader should be left in no doubt that Something

Must Be Done. All that remains is to bring them round to your view of precisely *what* should be done.

Possibilities

■ ■ ■

You may or may not want to consider different options for resolving the problem that your reader is now convinced exists. Or rather, the reader may or may not want to consider them – that's the factor that should determine whether or not you include a 'possibilities' section in your proposal. The reader is likely to be adopting one of two stances:

1 They will decide whether to do *x*, *y* or *z*.

2 They will either accept your proposal or leave things as they are.

In the first of these situations, the reader will consider other options whether you do or not. If you own a car wash, say, any potential customer will consider the options of using your car wash, washing their car themselves, getting the kid round the corner to do it for 50p, or leaving it dirty. You may only be offering one of the four options, but you'll need to discuss the other three with your customers in order to convince them that your option is better.

So if you're writing a proposal for a customer who is likely to be considering other options, you'll need to include a 'possibilities' section in order to discuss them. Or if the board is considering your proposal for restructuring, but also considering a more minor restructure, or the option of leaving things alone – you'll need to cover these options in your report.

However, if your reader is simply going to say yes or no, then there's no need to consider alternatives. If you're asking your bank manager for a loan for a new business you're starting,

they won't be choosing between yours and someone else's –
they'll give you both a loan if you both warrant one. It's a
straight yes or no choice; you can't very well include a section
on their other options when there aren't any.

Content

This section should cover the pros and cons of each possibility,
such as:

- how each one works or what it does (if the reader
  doesn't know)

- what it costs

- other relevant details such as how long it takes to
  implement, technical specifications etc.

- what its benefits are (it's the cheapest, it's very safe,
  customers seem to love it, it only takes two people to
  operate it etc.)

- what its disadvantages are (delivery takes four months,
  the staff hate using it, there's no absolute guarantee it
  will work and so on).

You may want to look at these factors for each option in isola-
tion, but you will probably also want to compare them. Don't
draw any overall conclusions at this stage – that comes later.
You may have your own preferred possibility but it shouldn't
be visible to the reader at this stage. You must describe all the
possibilities fairly and impartially.

Proposal
■ ■ ■

If you aren't including a 'possibilities' section this will probably be the largest part of the document. It will include:

- An explanation of what you are proposing (your business plan, for example, for your bank manager).

44

- Answers to any objections which you anticipate from your readers (such as the bank manager saying 'But why do you need as much as £25000?').

- Facts and figures to support your case (such as research showing there is a market gap for your proposed product).

If you have listed the 'possibilities', you will already have covered these points. In this case, the 'proposal' section should read a bit like the television *Call My Bluff* show: 'I don't think it's the first one; it sounded rather implausible. A sort of medieval alarm clock? I think not...' – that sort of thing. Except that you don't want to be rude about any of the options – but we'll look at that more closely in Chapter 6.

You've already discussed the pros and cons of each option under 'possibilities', so now you simply make a choice and justify it: 'All in all the brick house looks like the best option. The straw one will blow over too easily and the wood one, while it is slightly more stable, is nevertheless also vulnerable to fire. The brick one, on the other hand, should withstand any amount of wind and it won't burn. It's true that it's the most expensive, but its durability means that in the long term, say ten years, it's actually the cheapest of the three options. What's more, it's the only one that's truly secure against wolves, as the survey figures show.'

45

EXERCISE

Your turn again. Write a very brief proposal summary using the four 'P's – about one line to each section – for the following:

1 To persuade someone living without any power supply to have their house wired for electricity:

Position:

Problem:

46

Possibilities:

Proposal:

2 To persuade a young child to swallow nasty-tasting medicine:

Position:

Problem:

Possibilities:

Proposal:

RESPONSE

1 To persuade someone living without any power supply to have their house wired for electricity:

Position: You live in a house which is not connected to any mains power supply.

Problem: This means you have no hot water, no heating in winter and no strong light for reading, writing or other close-up work.

Possibilities: You could stay as you are, you could install a private power supply, you could connect up to mains gas, or you could put in electricity.

Proposal: The older you get, the harder it will become to cope without heating. A private supply can be hard work and more difficult to repair if things go wrong and mains gas can be expensive in a rural area. So I recommend you install mains electricity which is the cleanest, and the cheapest given your location.

47

2 To persuade a young child to swallow nasty-tasting medicine:

Position: You've got 'flu.

Problem: It makes you feel miserable, you've got a dreadful cough and a sore throat, your nose is bunged up and you feel hot and sweaty.

Possibilities: You could wait for it to go away, you could drink hot lemon and honey, or you could take this medicine.

Proposal: If you don't take anything you'll feel ill for much longer. If you take honey and lemon your throat will feel a bit better but the rest of you will be just as bad. So I suggest you take the medicine: it will only taste horrible for a short time, taking the medicine isn't as bad as having the 'flu, and you'll start to feel better almost straight away.

Summary

The four 'P's:

1 *Position: where we are now*

- Make sure you're all agreed on what the proposal is about.

- State the position from the reader's point of view.

2 *Problem: why we can't stay here*

- Could be good or bad.

- Persuade the reader that things can't be left as they are.

3 *Possibilities: all the places we could go instead*

- include this section unless the reader will be making a straight yes/no decision.

- discuss the pros and cons of each option, and draw comparisons between them where this is useful.

4 *Proposal: the best direction to choose*

- If you don't have a 'possibilities' section: explain your proposal, answer any objections and provide facts to support your case.

- If you do have a 'possibilities' section: make a choice and justify it.

5
■ ■ ■

Structure II: Reports

How could you use the four 'P's from the last chapter to structure your monthly management report? With difficulty, frankly. The four 'P's make the ideal structure when you are making recommendations – in other words for writing proposals. But the formula doesn't work for reports. That's what this chapter is about.

The structure is the only difference between writing reports and writing proposals. You set the objective and collect the information in the same way. And areas such as the use of English and the layout of the document are exactly the same. But the different functions of proposals and reports, which we considered in Chapter 1, dictate different structures.

Reports fall into two main categories – research reports and reports which simply impart information. These 'information only' reports include:

- updates
- memos (which don't include recommendations)
- regular reports such as budget reports and management reports.

The two categories of report – research, and information only – call for differing structures, so we'll look at them separately.

Research reports

■ ■ ■

You could be researching the market, researching new product ideas, researching options for how best to invest your reserves – hundreds of research reports get written every week. They're often vitally important; success or failure could hinge on your report. Your own success or failure as well as the company's – people will remember that you were the one who wrote that brilliant market report which led to the launch of their most successful product line. Conversely, people also remember those who are incapable of producing logical, readable, well-written reports.

Did you do chemistry at school? I remember the first experiment we ever did when I was about 11. We were heating water over a Bunsen burner to find out how fast sugar dissolved in it at different temperatures. While we were doing it we had to take lots of readings and make notes. Once we'd finished we had to write up the experiment. For the next five years this was standard procedure – you always had to write up the experiment afterwards and you always had to write it up in the same way: Aim, Method, Results, Conclusion.

1 **The Aim** was always a single sentence stating what you were trying to achieve, explain, discover or observe.

2 **The Method** was fairly brief and explained exactly what you had done and how you did it. I always thought it read a bit like a recipe – 'take 1oz sugar, dissolve in half a cup of water . . .'.

3 **The Results** told you what had happened. Obviously in this instance they simply reported the facts, without opinion or subjective judgement (this was chemistry, after all).

4 **The Conclusion** had a slightly more liberated feel than

the result – you were allowed to say what you thought, based of course on the facts, and it always had to refer back to the Aim at the beginning: 'So what we achieved/discovered/
observed was...'.

A chemistry experiment is, of course, a form of research. So it's not surprising that the structure for writing it up afterwards is actually the standard structure for writing any research report (I knew all those chemistry lessons had to be teaching me something useful).To explain exactly what I mean, I'll show you how the sugar-dissolving experiment goes. It may seem rather basic but structuring a research report, once you've learnt the formula, isn't difficult. And, as often happens, the simple skills we learn as kids are worth remembering because they form the basis of many of the more complex techniques we learn later.

51

Aim (you'll have realised, of course, that this is the objective we saw how to set in Chapter 2). To establish the effect of temperature on the length of time it takes for sugar to dissolve in water.

Method
We put exactly 1oz of sugar into half a beaker of water at room temperature (15°C) and stirred it continuously with a glass rod. Using a stopwatch we measured the time it took for the sugar to dissolve (the point at which we could no longer see any of the granules). We then repeated the process with the water at 30°C, 70°C and 100°C.

Results
At 15°C the sugar took 1 minute 53 seconds to dissolve.
At 30°C the sugar took 1 minute 10 seconds to dissolve.
At 70°C the sugar took 22 seconds to dissolve.
At 100°C the sugar took 5 seconds to dissolve.

Conclusion

Temperature affects the speed at which sugar dissolves in water. The hotter the water, the faster the sugar dissolves.

That was a reasonably brief experiment to describe. A research report could take considerably longer, perhaps including the formula for the correlation between speed and temperature. So could a more sophisticated chemistry experiment, no doubt – but this experiment still contains all the key ingredients.

Aim

The 'aim' should be equivalent to the objective that you set in Chapter 2. In a proposal (or an information only report) you would not necessarily include this in the final report – it's more for your use than the reader's. But in a research report you should include it. For example:

> 'The aim of our research was to establish the means by which cat owners judge which food their cats prefer and to find out how important the taste of the food is to the success of the product.'

Method

The 'method' you would use for a research report would include any of the ways of collecting information that we considered in Chapter 3. You might also conduct experiments if you were testing different materials, for example, to decide which to manufacture your products from – or you might use published reports of other people's experiments. You might test drive different vans to decide what to buy for your new fleet of vehicles, or use cats to taste different tins of food and see if you could tell which they liked best. So your 'method' section might read:

> 'In the first part of the test we interviewed 50 cat owners,

asking them all the same five questions (see Appendix for list of questions). We then put equal quantities of our new cat food and the cat's usual brand in separate (identical) bowls, brought the cat into the room and allowed it to eat whichever it preferred. We observed the cat's behaviour. The owner stayed in the room. We then asked the owner another five questions (see Appendix).

The second part of the test involved the same owners and cats and we followed the same procedure. However, this time we told the owners that we were using a different cat food (although we were not). We described this 'second' cat food as containing the ingredients which the owner had told us before were their cat's 'favourite.'

Results

The 'results', like the 'possibilities' section in a proposal, should not offer any opinion but should simply record what happened, how many interviewees said this or that, how easily each fabric tore, or the technical merits and disadvantages of each van that you tested. This is not the section for drawing comparisons, although the results can be presented in a form which allows them to be measured against each other. For example:

'In part one of the test, 68% of the cats ate most or all of both bowls of food. 18% declined to eat from either bowl. Of the remaining 14%, half ate their usual food and half ate our new brand.'

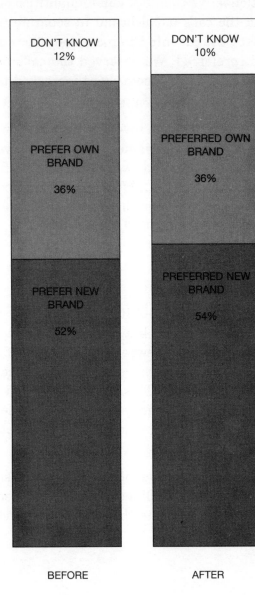

DON'T KNOW
12%

PREFER OWN
BRAND

36%

PREFER NEW
BRAND

52%

DON'T KNOW
10%

PREFERRED OWN
BRAND

36%

PREFERRED NEW
BRAND

54%

BEFORE

AFTER

54

Before the product testing 36% of owners thought their cat would prefer its usual brand of food to our new product, 12% didn't know and 52% thought the cat would prefer the new food. After watching the test 54% thought that the cat had preferred our new food. All 88% of owners who had made a prediction felt that the test had borne out their view.

All but 10% of owners believed they knew which food their cat had preferred, whether it had eaten one bowl or both, or not eaten either. They were asked afterwards how they judged what their cat's preference was, and the most frequent answers were:

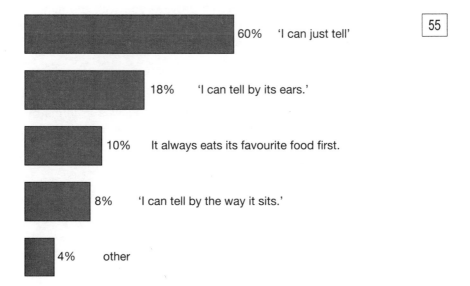

60%   'I can just tell'

18%   'I can tell by its ears.'

10%   It always eats its favourite food first.

8%   'I can tell by the way it sits.'

4%   other

Conclusion

The 'conclusion', like the chemistry experiment, should refer back to the objective, or aim, at the beginning. This is the place for making deductions or expressing views based on the results:

'It appears that the majority of cat owners believe that they know their cat's tastes extremely well, and buy food on the basis of this knowledge. The cat's response to the food appears to be less important than the owner's knowledge that their cat 'loves kidney' or 'can't stand jelly'. This suggests that the taste of the food (as long as the cat will actually eat it) is of secondary importance to the product's success. More important would be to find out what ingredients the majority of owners believe their cats like and to design a product based on this recipe.'

EXERCISE

Produce a brief market research report on the same lines as the chemistry experiment above. I'll provide you with the aim, so you know what your objective is. Keep it reasonably brief and choose your own method, results and conclusion – the important thing is to get the structure right.

Aim

To identify the best material for building beehives in terms of cost, durability and the taste of the honey; the options under consideration were wood, MDF and fibreglass.

Method

Results

Conclusion

RESPONSE

Don't worry about the precise content – especially if you're not an apiarist. Read through the response and make sure that you've included the right kind of information in each section of the report.

Aim

To identify the best material for building beehives out of in terms of cost, durability and the taste of the honey; the options under consideration were wood, MDF (Medium Density Fibreboard) and fibreglass.

Method

First we researched the cost of each of the three materials, taking into account the production costs, since the methods of production would vary.

Next, we built two prototype beehives out of each of the three materials. We subjected one beehive of each material to a high level of wear to assess its durability.

We kept bees in each of the second prototypes. All three hives were kept close together, and the bees all fed on the same pollen. We invited a panel of experts in the field – leading honey producers and apiarists – to taste each of the three honeys and comment on them.

Results

The cost of building 20 beehives a week was as follows:

Material	Cost each @ 20 per week
Wood	£50.23
MDF	£43.50
Fibreglass	£43.38

All three beehives withstood rough treatment, including being dropped, very well. The fibreglass one was the least resistant to wind, but the most resistant to water. It was the only one which was susceptible to condensation. There was no significant difference in performance between the beehive made out of MDF and the one made of wood.

The tasting showed that the honey from the wood and MDF hives was identical, and sweeter than the honey from the fibreglass hives, though the panel could not agree on which of the two tastes they preferred.

Conclusion
The MDF and wood beehives performed the same. In terms of cost, however, the fibreglass and MDF hives are the most economical to produce (in numbers of 20 or more a week). However, the fibreglass hives are less resistant to wind and the condensation could be a problem. The taste of the honey doesn't seem to be a relevant factor as no one honey was preferred to any other.

Altogether these results suggest that MDF is the best material to make beehives from since it is the most cost effective, and performs as well, if not better than, wood and fibreglass in terms of durability and taste.

Never mind if you turned out to be wrong about the best kind of hive. Actually, I was only guessing.

That's really all you need to know to structure a research report. Just think 'chemistry': Aim, Method, Results, Conclusion. There's only one more thing to mention: occasionally you may be asked to research and write a report *with recommendations*. Great. So what's that when it's at home? A proposal or a research report?

I can't tell you – because it varies. But I can tell you how to work it out for yourself. Think about it from the point of view of the person who asked you to write it:

1 If the reason they want the document is in order to make a specific decision at the end, for a specific purpose, it's a proposal. For instance the intention might be that they are going to choose option A: build our next batch of beehives from MDF.

2 On the other hand, if they merely want the report and its conclusions for reference – perhaps frequent and important reference, but not relating to one specific decision – it is a report with recommendations. For

example, they may want to know about materials for building beehives for future decisions. Maybe they're considering the possibility of introducing a cheaper line, and thinking about streamlining the production system, so this report will come in handy for several decisions.

Information only reports

Now for the good news. If you're writing a report simply to pass on information – a memo, a monthly departmental report or whatever – you've already structured it. The fact is that there is no particular way of putting this kind of report together that makes it any easier to read and understand.

60

You'll remember that when we collected the facts together in Chapter 3 we organised them into logical groups. For an information only report, this is as far as you need to go. If you set out the information by simply working through these groups in order, you're being as clear and helpful to your readers as you can be.

Putting the groups in order

Sometimes you may find that there is a sensible order in which to deal with the groups, in which case of course you should use it. So if you've organised your information by date you will probably go through it chronologically, working either forwards or backwards depending on which is more suitable. But if you've grouped the information by department it probably doesn't make any difference what order you work through them in.

EXERCISE

How many different ways of ordering the groups can you think of –
such as by date, or by department – which you could use for an
information only report?

RESPONSE

It's impossible to give an exhaustive list of ways to put the groups
into order, but here are some ideas:

■ by date

■ in order of importance

■ working through the products in the same order as the catalogue

■ working through branches or divisions in order of size, turnover or
location

You may sometimes find that you have a choice of logical
routes through the information. If this happens, use
whichever you're most comfortable with. The key thing to
remember is that the point of using a considered structure,
rather than simply putting the information down in any
order it comes to hand, is to help the reader to:

■ take it in as quickly as possible

■ follow it easily

■ understand it

■ remember it.

As long as you're achieving that, you're doing fine.

Summary

1 *Research reports*

Structure into four sections:

- Aim
- Method
- Results
- Conclusion

2 *Information only reports*

- Present the information in the logical groups you put it into when you collected it.
- If possible, work through these groups in a logical order.

6

■ ■ ■

The power of persuasion

You know what you're going to say, and you know the order in which you are going to say it. But before we look at the precise words and phrases you're going to use, which we'll do in the next chapter, there's one more thing to consider. Selling.

All proposals are sales documents, as are many reports; even if your customer is internal and not external you're still selling your idea – your way of doing things – to the boss, the Board of Directors or whoever. And selling is all about persuading people to see things from a particular perspective which will convince them to buy, or adopt the scheme, or agree the purchase or whatever it is you want your proposal to achieve.

Deep down, most of us are like small children, only bigger. You know that if you want a small child to do something they've never done before, they're far more likely to agree to it if you tell them that it will be exciting and fun than if you tell them to do it 'because I say so'. Customers, Managing Directors and the like are much the same – we all are. And the same techniques which are effective with children tend to be just as effective with grown-ups. It's absolutely vital to learn to use these techniques in proposals and reports if we're going to get the results we want.

There are two key stages in persuading people round to your way of thinking:

1 Show you're on their side

2 Lead them over to your side.

The psychology
■ ■ ■

The process of reading a report or proposal is more emotional (albeit unconsciously) than you might think. The reader needs to feel that you understand their position. In a sense, it shows that you accept them, it puts you both on the same team. This feeling of acceptance is surprisingly important, even to the most hard-bitten business people. We looked at expressing the objective from the reader's point of view earlier, and this is a large part of the reason; you've got to show that you're starting in their camp. Even if you disagree with the reader's current attitude to the decision in question.

In other words, you have to start by convincing the reader that you're on their side. Anything else would antagonise them, obviously, because the implication would be that their judgement was not as good as yours and nobody wants to hear that. When you say to a small child 'because I say so', you're telling them that you know more than them and that your opinion is more important than theirs. No wonder they get annoyed. But when you say to them 'go on – it'll be fun and exciting' you're saying that you understand what they want, and their judgement is valid – it's OK to want to do fun, exciting things. You're on their side.

Once you're standing alongside your reader – they've accepted you and they're confident that you've accepted them – you can gently start to lead them where you want them to go. You can explain things from their perspective and guide them towards the right decision. They're much more likely to listen to you when you're standing next to them. If you were miles away shouting 'Come over here – it's much nicer, honest!' they could reasonably ask 'How do you know? You don't know what it's like over here.'

	Readers position	Your option
Stage 1	Reader	You
Stage 2	Reader You	
Stage 3	You Reader	
Stage 4		Reader You

65

So that's the key to the psychology. Don't stand in your entrenched position shouting 'Come here!' If you want them to agree to your proposal, you have to do the work. Go over to them, take their hand and lead them back to your position.

All the techniques in this chapter are ways of convincing the reader that you're on their side, or guiding them back to your side without losing them *en route*. Some of them are more applicable to proposals than reports, since proposals are specifically intended to persuade, so I shall mostly refer to proposals in this chapter. However, the techniques apply to reports as well; and indeed to presentations, meetings, letter writing – and dealing with small children.

Show you're on their side
■ ■ ■

This half of the process applies to every report or proposal you write. However, for a lot of reports you are genuinely on the same side as your reader to start with so this is automatic. Even so, it never hurts to double check that you're following the guidelines. For proposals, as we've seen, it's imperative.

Write from the reader's point of view

Imagine you're on the receiving end. It's much harder to bring yourself to agree with someone who clearly doesn't see things your way – who wants to satisfy their own needs and not yours. I once had a phone call from an estate agent who said: 'I've got your name on our mailing list – are you still looking for a house?' I replied, 'I don't think so. I've seen a house through another agent that looks just right and I've put in an offer.' The estate agent replied 'Oh no. What a shame!'

She then went on to ask me to let her know if it fell through. I no longer felt, however, that she actually wanted the same thing as me at all. I wanted to find a house that met my needs. She wanted me to find a house which gave her a commission.

Actually, if we think about it we know perfectly well that's what all estate agents want. But we tend to suppress that knowledge – we let ourselves believe that the estate agent just wants us to be happy. If you're an estate agent you don't actually have the huge task of convincing your customer that you're more interested in their happiness than in your own wages. All you have to do is to show that you're looking at it from their point of view. Just say 'Congratulations – I hope it works out.' It makes them feel that you understand and accept their position.

It's important to put yourself in the reader's position from the very beginning. The *position* and *problem* sections of the proposal are the place to establish this rapport. Always describe their position and their problem, and make it clear that you accept it as such. Never give the impression (even if it's the truth) that you don't see their problem as a problem at all.

Suppose the board has asked you to write a proposal. Let's say they're not happy with the cost of the food in the canteen; they think it's unnecessary to provide such a wide range at such a generous subsidy. You, on the other hand, think it's the least they can do for their hard-working and loyal staff.

You should still explain the problem as they see it. Once you do that, they'll feel you're on their side; so they're far more likely to believe you when you explain later on that, unfortunately, any change in the arrangements would lead to more problems than it would solve.

67

Show you understand the real issues

No-one is going to take your advice if they think you don't understand what's going on. So make sure you not only establish what the key factors are for the reader, but actively demonstrate that you understand.

So if you're trying to sell the town council one of your adventure playgrounds for the local park, find out if there's a particular reason why they're interested, or a special area of concern. Normally you can find out simply by asking them. Perhaps they're trying to allocate the budget before a certain date; maybe they want to build a new complex on one of the other parks and they think they will reduce the outcry if people prefer this park anyway. Or perhaps the neighbouring town council has just built an adventure playground and it has boosted their popularity.

Sometimes, as in the last of those three examples, you want the readers to see that you understand the issue but you don't really want to suggest that you know they're spending public money to boost their own popularity. You don't have to. The trick is to mention the issue in some other context – show you know about it without letting on that you know their motives. You could say, for example: 'The evidence shows that people approve of their taxes being spent on improvements for the local children. In the next town, for example, the new adventure playground was greeted enthusiastically, and 78 per cent of townspeople surveyed said it was an asset to the town.'

EXERCISE

You have to write a proposal on a subject about which you know very little. List as many different ways as you can think of in which you could find out whether there are any central issues which you haven't already uncovered:

1 For internal readers (such as the Board, your boss, the Regional Director etc.): a proposal to put a fitness centre/gymnasium in the car parking area.

2 For external customers: a proposal to take over the whole contract for maintenance, redecoration and landscaping of their factory, currently being done by separate firms.

RESPONSE

1 For internal readers

■ Ask them – just because you don't know about a certain factor, it doesn't automatically mean you're not supposed to. If you ask 'Is there anything that I might not know about which is relevant?' they
could well say 'You've heard about the launch being brought forward, have you?'

■ Think – especially if they have said anything that you couldn't see a reason for, or asked you to cover topics you wouldn't have expected to deal with. For example, you could ask why they want to consider building on the car park specifically, rather than con-sidering any other options.

■ Read minutes of recent meetings if you can.

■ Read your annual report.

■ Talk to your colleagues and your boss.

■ Talk to *their* colleagues.

■ Talk to key people in other relevant departments. Personnel may know better than you what's being planned for future car parking, for example.

■ The research you do into fitness centres and gymnasiums may guide you towards certain key questions which will ascertain if there are any other issues to learn about – you might find grantsare available for capital improvements for the benefit of employees. Or that one of the re ommended suppliers is owned by one of your company's non-executive directors.

2 For external customers

■ Ask them.

■ Think. Put yourself in the reader's shoes and think through the areas you're covering in the report. What would matter most to them?

■ Look through back issues of their trade publications.

■ Read their annual report and their customer newsletter.

- If they have an internal newsletter see if you can get hold of a copy.

- Is there anyone else in their company you can talk to? If you're writing a sales proposal for their Marketing Director, you might have a good, long-standing relationship with their Administration Manager. Can they tell you anything?

- Talk to other suppliers (excluding your own competitors). What about the people who do their office cleaning – could they tell you anything useful?

- Talk to your colleagues and your boss, especially if they also deal with the same customer, or others in the same industry.

Be objective

Your own credibility is vital. No-one is going to allow you to lead them round to your way of thinking if they don't trust your judgement. So you need to make it very clear that you are judging the facts objectively. If the data suggested a different route you would take it; you're only recommending your own product because you genuinely consider that it matches the criteria more closely than the others: that's the feeling you want your readers to come away with. It's usually true, in fact. If you don't think you're recommending the best option – why are you doing it? There are two important ways to make sure you appear objective:

- Don't use value judgements.
- Prefer hard facts to unsupported assertions.

Don't use value judgements

Avoid subjective words like 'best' – choose an objective alternative. Say it's the 'fastest' or the 'most accurate'; these are statements you can prove. Keep away from fancy adjectives – 'its incredible speed' or 'stunning performance'. It's far more persuasive to specify: 'speeds up to 120 mph' or 'performance which, in tests, was consistently 6 per cent above its nearest rival'.

If you can use these objective measures you will carry far more clout. It doesn't sound as if you have a vested interest; you're simply stating the facts. If you have no objective measure, don't use subjective statements as an alternative – if you're asked to justify them you'll find yourself in trouble.

Prefer hard facts to unsupported assertions

If you want to say that your idea, product or whatever is the most exciting, the cheapest or the longest lasting, *always* back it up. Equally, if you want to suggest that any other option is less reliable, needs more maintenance or doesn't come in such nice colours, use supporting data to justify your argument.

71

If you can't find – or commission – the data you need, don't include the fact. If you *can't* back it up it really isn't a fact anyway, it's an opinion or a supposition. There are degrees of certainty in this kind of information, of course. You might be able to say anything from 'seven independent tests, four of them conducted live on prime time television, showed conclusively that. . .' to 'initial tests haven't been completed yet, but the early findings indicate that . . .'. The more conclusive, the better. But any legitimate support is is better than nothing.

You might be wondering how you can support a statement that something is 'more exciting' than the competition, or 'comes in nicer colours'; especially if you're not supposed to be subjective. Well, it's your own personal opinion you shouldn't express. But if you've conducted surveys which show that 95 per cent of children who had tried your adventure playground said it was the most exciting they'd ever been on – that's fine. That's an objective statement; it is a fact that 95 per cent of them said it.

Make sure that you never make any assertions which you

can't justify. You might decide to put the supporting informa-tion in an appendix, you might choose not even to include it in the final document at all, but if asked for it, you must be able to produce it.

Lead them over to your side

■ ■ ■

So now, at the end of the *position* and *problem* sections, you're standing shoulder to shoulder with your reader. They know you understand their situation and their needs. You have shown them your judgement is sound and your information accurate. Now it's time to examine the *possibilities*. This is where you start to lead the reader back over to your side. But do it as carefully as if you were treading on eggshells.

Be fair

Treat all the options fairly. If one of the other possibilities works out cheaper than the one you're recommending, don't attempt to hide the fact. It's not worth the risk of being found out – which you almost certainly will. If your readers spot you omitting important data, or trying to mislead them, not only have you lost your credibility for this particular proposal, but probably for all future proposals too. Even if the reader does-n't spot it now, they may do after they've made the decision and started to use your equipment, drive your cars or operate your recommended pension fund.

A false statement or the suppression of a relevant fact is like the thirteenth chime of a clock: it isn't just obviously wrong in itself, it also casts doubt on the previous 12.

Furthermore, if this is a proposal to a customer and you make a derogatory comment about one of your competitors, the cus-tomer is unlikely to believe you anyway. Their response will simply be 'Well they would say that, wouldn't they?' And if they already use your competitor's product they will feel you are insulting their judgement. If, on the other hand, the readers see you being scrupulously fair, they will have far more faith in your judgement, and be happy to follow you to whatever conclusion you decide to lead them.

Just because you're being fair, however, you don't have to draw attention to any weak points in your own product. All the facts should be there, but you can choose how to present them. Suppose you're listing cost comparisons between all the possible options, and your preference happens to be the most expensive. You can't lie, and you can't very well omit to discuss the cost, but you can at least make sure that you don't list the price immediately next to the cheapest option. There's no point drawing attention to it.

73

Don't pooh-pooh the other possibilities

Your readers will consider all the possibilities to be viable options. That's why you're listing them. If someone wants to soft boil an egg for their breakfast and is deciding how long to cook it for, you might suggest three minutes, four minutes, four and a half, or five. But you're not going to bother suggesting they get up at 5 o'clock in the morning, coat it in wax so it can't breathe and leave it in the sun for three hours while they go back to bed. You know that option isn't in the running.

Never forget that your readers are giving serious consideration to all the other possibilities. So, by criticising any of the options, however subtly, you are in effect insulting their judgement. That doesn't mean you have to flatter the alternatives to your idea – simply remain objective about them. This helps to convince the reader that you're on their side – like them, you too are considering the alternatives.

Give the readers an excuse to change their minds

Suppose you're putting a proposal to half a dozen or more

people. Some of them may already have expressed strong views on the subject of your proposal. Perhaps they've been arguing fiercely that the adventure playground can't possibly have a rope slide because it's far too dangerous while you are recommending that it should have a rope slide. You know enough about what people are like (we're back to the psychology again) – they don't like backing down. So give them an excuse. Explain that safety should be the number one priority and rope slides are traditionally thought to be dangerous, but your new, double locking harness with safety release has vastly reduced both the risk and the maximum level of injury possible.

You've now given them an excuse to come round to your view without losing face. They can say 'You see; I was right. Rope slides do have a very poor safety record. But of course, if there's new technology now, that could make a difference . . .'.

Put your preferred option last

Your approach to the possibilities you've laid out may vary. For a sales proposal it may well be that the only option you'll be happy with is the one you're recommending – or you may hope that if they don't buy your top-of-the range vans they will buy the middle-range ones, rather than going to another supplier. If you're presenting an internal report with recommendations you might have a first choice, but with several other options that you consider to be perfectly acceptable.

So don't back yourself into a corner by making one clear recommendation if there are others which you would settle for. But whether you're pointing up your number one choice subtly or obviously, put it last. That way it's freshest in your readers' minds when they start to read the recommendations.

Anticipate objections

If you're in a meeting, or giving a presentation, you can ask the person you're talking to if they have any comments or questions. But on paper you don't have that opportunity, so you have to work out in advance what comments or questions they might have so you can make sure you deal with them.

If there's a chance that they might object to the price of your adventure playground, for example, you can point out that:

- Because it's so sturdy, it won't need repairing or replacing as quickly as most, so what you spend on the playground you'll save on maintenance and repair bills.

- Surveys show that it's popular enough to charge an entrance fee for or, as many councils do, you can set up an ice cream or sweet stall nearby and offset the price with the income from renting out the stall.

- You can save money by closing down two or three older playgrounds in the locality, as the kids will prefer to use this one.

There are lots of other possible justifications to answer the price objection. The point is to anticipate the problem areas and come up with legitimate compensating factors – which you can support with facts. Put the objection in perspective – your product may be a little more expensive, but the price is all-in and includes several extras that the other options do not.

You don't want to draw attention to an objection the reader hasn't thought of, or provide ammunition for the one dissenter on the board; but you can answer an objection without directly mentioning it. If you look at the three price justifications above, you'll notice that none of them makes direct reference to the fact that the price is high.

Just occasionally, however, you can break this rule – normally if it's obvious that the reader is bound to have thought of the objection. You could say something like 'If you want the cheapest solution irrespective of accuracy and durability then Superlux Chronometers are not the answer. But if you value performance . . .'.

EXERCISE

Take the example of the adventure playground. Try to think of two or three compensating factors to answer each of the following potential objections. Remember not to draw attention to the objection.

1 'It takes up too much space.'

2 'It takes too long to deliver and erect.'

3 'It's got far more features than we need.'

4 'It's not safe; we need swings and roundabouts, not 20 foot high nets and rope slides.'

RESPONSE

1 'It takes up too much space.'

■ The whole site is about 20 metres square; anything smaller would be a safety risk.

■ The site will take up around 10 per cent of the total area of the park. According to other councils' experience, it will attract more like 50 per cent of the visitors to the park.

■ The fact that the site occupies about 10 per cent of the park means that parents can enjoy the rest of the park while their children play, without ever being out of sight or out of earshot.

2 'It takes too long to deliver and erect.'

■ We make every playground to order. It may take a little longer but that's not usually a problem, and it means we can customise each separate feature in any way you choose.

■ Once we've built the playground, we spend two weeks safety testing all the equipment before we deliver it to site.

■ The erection of the playground is very thorough. We bury all the supporting uprights in a minimum of six feet of concrete and we do a full safety survey of any trees which are being incorporated into the playground. When we've finished we test the equipment again and then we use a special technique to soften the surface of the ground to minimise injuries in the event of a fall.

3 'It's got far more features than we need.'

- Twelve separate features is probably the optimum number, judging by other buyers' experiences. The playgrounds are very popular, especially during school holidays, and if the kids have to queue for hours to have a go on their favourite swing or slide they get fractious, and the attraction of the playground loses its appeal.

- Adventure playgrounds are healthy for kids. Each feature here exercises a different set of muscles, or builds their strength or aerobic fitness. This combination of a dozen features is the minimum number required to give kids the chance to develop all-round fitness.

- In surveys, these 12 features lead the field in popularity. This selection covers the basics which children expect these days – one slide, one swing, one walkway and so on.

4 'It's not safe; we need swings and roundabouts, not 20 feet high nets and rope slides.'

- Some kids aren't happy unless they're 20 feet above ground. They're the ones who climb trees if we *don't* give them an adventure playground. This is an ideal way to keep them happy and safe because here they have handrails and safety harnesses too.

- Our adventure playgrounds have a better safety record than traditional playgrounds. It's obvious that safety has to be a top priority, so we invest a lot of money in it. Every slide, climbing frame and walkway in the playground has at least two safety features built in as standard.

This is your key opportunity to promote your favoured option, if you have one. At the point where you say 'I recommend the twelve-feature adventure playground because . . .' you can finally start to argue your case thoroughly. This is the first and only opportunity to discuss your recommendation in a different light from all the rest. You can give your own choice a treatment that you don't give the others:

- list all its best points
- link any apparent weaknesses with compensating factors. ('It's not the cheapest, but it is the most durable.')

In a sales proposal which has not listed other possibilities this section will take up most of the document.

If you have expressed all the relevant points objectively, fairly and honestly, shown respect for all the options, given the *readers* an excuse to change their minds and anticipated all the objections – you have maximised your chances of bringing the *readers* over to your side. If this doesn't persuade them, nothing will.

79

Summary

1 *Show them you're on their side*

- Write from the reader's point of view
- Show you understand the real issues
- Be objective

2 *Lead them over to your side*

- Be fair
- Don't pooh-pooh the other possibilities
- Give the reader an excuse to change their mind
- Put your preferred option last
- Anticipate objections

7
■ ■ ■

Using plain English I: Style

Many people find it easy to talk clearly and coherently, but as soon as you put a pen in their hand they become nervous, verbose or develop a need to 'impress' with long words and complex sentences. No matter how well a report is structured and thought out, its power to persuade or inform will be diluted if the language is unclear.

The use of English falls into two main categories:

1 Style.

2 Mechanics.

This chapter will examine the style of your proposal or report – the overall approach – and Chapter 8 will look at the Mechanics – the grammar and syntax.

We'll start with the general approach or tone of the document, before moving on to the details of the phrasing and sentences we use. Finally we'll consider the individual words we choose.

General approach
■ ■ ■

Match the style to the reader

If you were at school 40 years ago, you were probably taught to use words like 'whomever', to make sure every sentence had a subject, a verb and an object, and *never* to say 'less' when you meant 'fewer'. Nowadays, writing as we speak is becoming more acceptable – it's OK now, for example, to write 'it's OK'.

However, we're writing our reports and proposals for our readers, not for ourselves. So think for a minute about what your readers' preferred style is. In this chapter and the next I'll be giving examples of the standard approach that is considered acceptable in the 1990s. It's the best style to use for about 85–90 per cent of readers, and it's usually not too far wrong for the rest. But if you're writing for certain types of reader, it might be better to tweak it slightly:

- **Old fashioned readers:** If your readers were at school 40 years ago, they may be fussier than you about 'correct' grammar. It still is *technically* correct, there is simply less emphasis on its importance. So you're probably better off using words like 'whomever', and giving every sentence a subject, a verb and an object. If you've never met your readers but you suspect they're old fashioned – perhaps they're a group of elderly barristers, for instance – steer away from the most obvious modern colloquialisms. And don't start sentences with 'and'.

- **Young readers:** Conversely, if you use words like 'whom' when you're writing for most young readers, you'll alienate them. Don't break the rules (outlined in the next chapter) but feel free to stretch them. The readers will feel you're on their wavelength.

■ **Readers with restricted reading skills:** Perhaps some of your readers are foreign and their English is poor. Or maybe the report is for your boss who is mildly dyslexic. If for any reason your readers might have problems with standard English, or with certain words, adapt your style to avoid any specific problem areas. If your readers don't speak good English, the ideal solution is to have the proposal or report translated. Failing that, however, it would be better to replace the word 'magnitude' with 'size', for instance, or 'archive' with 'records'.

Adapting your style to suit the reader is one of the best subliminal techniques for showing you're on their side – it makes them feel that you're their sort of a person.

83

Use everyday English

Vocabulary

As far as the other 85–90 per cent of readers are concerned, it's better to use idiomatic English. This is not the same thing as using slang. Try to write in the same way that you speak – it's much easier to read. So you don't have to refer to the w.c. as the washroom or toilet, you can call it the lavatory – exactly as you might if you were speaking to your reader. Just avoid slang words like 'bog'.

Elision

This means eliding, or running together, two or more words. In other words you can use words like:

■ 'isn't' instead of 'is not'
■ 'you've' instead of 'you have'

■ 'can't' instead of 'cannot'.

(This is probably better avoided with your more old fashioned readers.)

Use the first and second person

It's much friendlier and more colloquial to refer to yourself as
'I' (or 'we' if you're writing on behalf of a group or your company); it's what you'd say if you were speaking directly to the
reader. Equally, it's far better to call them 'you' as you would
in speech. So instead of saying 'it would appear that considerable expenditure will be needed . . .' you can say 'it seems to
us that you're going to have to spend quite a lot . . .'.

| 84 |

EXERCISE

Certain words sound very stilted and formal, and are better used
sparingly or avoided altogether. Try to suggest a better alternative for
each of the following examples.

Formal expression	*Alternative*
in respect of	
prior to	
remittance	
ascertain	
endeavour	
in the event of	
in consequence	
I have not commenced	
dwelling	
in excess of	
in lieu of	
persons	

utilise

terminate

I am in receipt of

RESPONSE

Formal expression	Alternative	Formal expression	Alternative
in respect of	about	dwelling	house
prior to	before	in excess of	more than
remittance	payment	in lieu of	instead of
ascertain	find out	persons	people
endeavour	try	utilise	use
in the event of	if	terminate	end, stop
in consequence	so	I am in receipt of	I've got
I have not commenced	I haven't started		

You tend to find that you don't need to learn to avoid each of these words and phrases individually, because it's simply a matter of style. That's why I've included it in this part of the chapter and not under the section on specific words – this is to do with your basic approach to using language. If your vocabulary is prone to change when you pick up a pen, you simply need to learn to write as you speak. Try this:

1 Write down in note form the points you want to make and the order you want to make them in.

2 Imagine the readers are in the room with you.

3 Stand up.

4 Turn on your dictaphone or tape recorder.

5 Talk through your notes as if you were giving a presentation.

This is the best way to ensure that you use idiomatic English, not formal language. Once this spoken version of your report is typed up, it should need surprisingly few changes.

Be politically correct

Whatever their view, this topic gets almost everybody incredibly heated. But it doesn't matter what *your* view is of course; it's the reader's view that counts. If you're in any doubt at all, don't take chances. The fact is that this particular subject is now so well discussed that anyone who doesn't follow the modern approach appears, at best, to be fuddy-duddy and out of touch. So make sure your reports and proposals are free of racism, ageism, sexism and any other -isms you can think of, regardless of your personal views.

86

Avoiding sexism

All the other subjects or words that are not politically correct (or 'PC') are pretty easy to avoid. But it can seem quite difficult to avoid any reference to gender except when talking about real people. So here are a few tips:

- Rewrite the sentence in the plural: instead of 'England expects that every man will do his duty' write 'England expects that everyone will do their duty'.

- It's now usually acceptable to use the pronoun 'they' in place of 'he' or 'she', so instead of 'Ask your boss if he or she wants a cup of tea' you can say 'Ask your boss if they want a cup of tea'. Occasionally this construction can sound uncomfortable, however, in which case use one of the alternative techniques to avoid referring to gender.

- You can use the phrase 'he or she' (or variations on it such as he/she or s/he). This can be intrusive, however, and tends to draw attention to itself. It's certainly correct, but it may not always be the smoothest approach.

■ Say 'you' or 'your'. For example, instead of saying 'every employee should leave his desk tidy' say 'leave your desk tidy'. Apart from being more correct, this is also a much friendlier style to adopt.

Explain new ideas clearly

You must know the old challenge: explain a spiral staircase without using your hands. Well, with reports and proposals you can never use your hands. Sometimes you can provide diagrams and drawings, but not if you're explaining an abstract concept. What's more, you won't be there when your readers see the document, so they can't stop you as they could at a presentation and ask you to run that one past them again.

87

Use examples

One or two clear examples can make all the difference between clarity and bafflement. For instance (you see, I'm giving you an example): I said earlier that it's OK to elide words in idiomatic writing. Now, if you didn't know what elide meant, you'd have been baffled. But as soon as I give you an example – 'isn't' instead of 'is not', or 'can't' instead of 'cannot' – it should become perfectly clear.

Never underestimate the value of giving examples. Something may be evident to you, but not necessarily so obvious to your readers. If you think there's any chance that the reader might benefit from an example, supply one.

Use metaphors and analogies

These are also invaluable devices, especially for explaining abstract concepts and ideas. I used a metaphor in the last chapter (here's another example). I said that the way to persuade someone to come round to your way of thinking was to 'show that you're on their side' and then 'lead them over to your side'. I was trying to explain an abstract concept, and the best way seemed to be to find a concrete visual image to relate it to.

You need to be careful to avoid mixed metaphors – chiefly because you run the risk of making a laughing stock of yourself. This simply means combining two or more different pieces of visual imagery which weren't designed to go together, such as describing headmasters as 'educational dinosaurs cloistered in their ivory towers'. Here are two genuine examples, both from journalists:

88

'After shooting himself in the foot last week he has now scored an own goal.'

'President Reagan has left a legacy that may yet turn sour in the mouths of those who rode to victory on it.'

Analogies tend to start 'it's a bit like . . .' or 'it's as if . . .'. Suppose you're trying to explain how white blood corpuscles work. You could say 'they're a bit like a school of pirahna, swimming gently along. As soon as anything alien appears in their river, they descend on it and attack it mercilessly until they've eaten it. Then they go back to drifting in the current again.'

The key thing with examples, metaphors and analogies is knowing when to use them. If you're in any doubt, ask a plain-speaking and honest colleague or friend to read your first draft and tell you if you need to explain anything more clearly. Obviously you need to ask someone whose knowledge of the subject is not substantially different from the readers.

If you're writing about a new drug for treating heart disease, and your readership is a group of senior consultants who specialise in cardiac disorders, there's no point asking someone who thinks their heart is somewhere on the right behind the lungs to read through it for you. They will need things explained that the doctors won't. Equally, if you're writing for heart patients, don't get the consultants to read it – they'll understand things which will baffle the patients completely. So find a volunteer whose knowledge roughly equates with that of your readers.

Phrasing and sentences
■ ■ ■

Avoid jargon

'MS/DOS'

'Distributor cap'

'Gearing ratio'

89

How would you define jargon? It's a specialised language relating to a particular subject. It's everyday speech to one person and confusing or unfamiliar terminology to the next. All the words above are jargon to some people.

There's nothing wrong with jargon in itself. The reason it exists is because it's a convenient shorthand when we're discussing a subject with other people in the know, and it's helpful and concise to use it in a report or proposal if all the readers are used to it. But it's vital to be aware of when we're using it, so we can avoid it if any of our readers are unfamiliar with it.

Just occasionally you really have to use jargon. Particularly in technical proposals and reports there can be times when there are no alternatives to jargon words. When this happens the best solution is to include a glossary in the report, explaining each word as fully as necessary (we'll cover glossaries in Chapter 10).

EXERCISE

Here's an exercise without a response box; there are no right and wrong answers. In the left hand column, write a list of the most common jargon words and phrases you use in your work – or words and phrases that could be considered jargon by somebody. Then, in the right hand column, write a non-jargonistic alternative which you could use when you're communicating with people who don't know so much about the subject.

Jargon | *Alternative*

This is a very useful exercise, because once you've worked out these alternatives you can have them on the tip of your tongue to use in meetings, at presentations, in letters and for all sorts of other communications.

Avoid stock phrases

How often do you hear people say 'at this precise moment in time'? What they mean is 'now'. For some reason the English language, and business English in particular, is full of this kind of cumbersome, often slightly pompous, phrase. These expressions:

- waste space
- give the reader time to lose the thread of the sentence
- make you sound like everyone else, and
- give the whole document a slightly woolly feel.

None of which does anything for your image as an original thinker and a dynamic manager.

91

EXERCISE

Go through these examples of overused stock phrases and find more succinct alternatives.

Phrase   *Alternative*

There is a reasonable expectation that . . .

Owing to the situation that . . .

Should a situation arise where . . .

Taking into consideration such factors as . . .

Prior to the occasion when . . .

RESPONSE

Phrase	Alternative
There is a reasonable expectation that . . .	Probably
Owing to the situation that . . .	Because, since
Should a situation arise where . . .	If
Taking into consideration such factors as . . .	Considering
Prior to the occasion when . . .	Before

92

Avoid clichés

There are certain phrases of a slightly different type which are commonly used in business and which have effectively lost their meaning through over use. The reader's eye skims over them because it has seen them so many times before. For example:

- meeting customer needs
- a wide range of products and services
- represents real value for money
- high quality at low prices.

These expressions all meant something once, but they've become so stale that they might as well not be there. The word 'quality' is a good example – no-one believes it because *everyone* claims it. Nowadays, if you want to convey the impression that your products are of a high standard you're obliged to do it by quoting hard facts – as we saw in the last chapter. Hang on, though – maybe that's not such a bad thing.

And that's the other reason for avoiding these clichés: almost invariably, there's a better way of saying the same thing. 'A wide range of products and services' – why not say what they are? Or at least give an idea: over 30 different vehicles, from two-door sports cars to four-ton trucks. It's much clearer, and gives the reader a concrete visual image.

Keep sentences and paragraphs short

Sentences

The longer your sentences, the harder your writing will be to read. Vary the length, but try to average about 20 words – that's enough to avoid the risk of being patronising or over-simplistic. You should rarely go above 35 words and try never to exceed 40.

93

If you vary the length of your sentences (without letting them get too long) it adds texture and rhythm to your writing. Short sentences, used sparingly, can have impact and make your writing lively and fun to read.

If you find that a lot of your sentences are too long, you can often shorten them by:

- splitting them into two or more shorter sentences
- removing any unnecessary words or phrases.

To give you an example, see how you would break up this sentence:

'In the event that invoices are returned to us by customers who are raising some form of query, they should be copied immediately and without delay; one copy should be sent to the sales departments and one to accounts and these two departments should then confer as to the cause of the problem and decide, according to this, which of them should contact the customer.'

There's more than one way of doing this, of course, but here's an example. The redundant words are printed in italic so you can see which words are being omitted. Added words are in brackets.

> '*In the event that* (If) invoices are returned *to us by cus-tomers who are raising* (with) some form of query, they should be copied immediately. *and without delay.* One copy should be sent to the sales departments and one to accounts. These two departments should then confer as to the cause of the problem and decide, *according to this,* which of them should contact the customer.'

That was one way of doing it – simply by deleting words and changing punctuation. You could, of course, have rewritten the sentence completely, retaining little but its meaning.

Paragraphs

We'll discuss layout in a later chapter, but apart from the visual benefits of short paragraphs, they also help the flow of the text. Each new idea should start a new paragraph; this signals to the reader that they're onto a new thought and makes it far easier to follow the thread of your argument.

Words
■ ■ ■

Use short words

Long words take longer to read and can block the flow of your writing. Some long words are unavoidable, and indeed to avoid them altogether would deprive your writing of texture and variety. But some long words are pointless: why say 'assistance' when you can say 'help'?

Long words which are familiar are easier to read than those which the reader doesn't see very often. So your brain can far more easily take in the word 'telecommunications' than 'picaresque', even though it's actually longer.

Avoid legal words and pomposity

Again these words make it harder you to run your eye smoothly down the page. Here is a selection of legal words to avoid:

forthwith	hereof	of the (4th) inst.	thereof
henceforth	hereto	thereat	whereat
hereat	herewith	therein	whereon

95

Legal-speak also has a habit of referring back to other parts of the text so you have to jump backwards and forwards to find what the reference is to. Often you can simply omit the word altogether:

'The said mechanical digger . . .' can be changed to 'The mechanical digger . . .'.

Failing that, you can replace the legal term with the thing to which it refers:

'The aforementioned companies have agreed . . .' can change to 'ABC Co. and XYZ Ltd. have agreed. . .'.

Avoid neutral words

The more expressive your language, the more interesting it will be to read. So try to replace neutral words and phrases like 'alter', 'affect' and 'express an opinion' with more specific ones. For instance you could replace 'his performance altered when he started to wear red' with 'his performance improved when he started to wear red', change 'she expressed an opinion' to 'she preferred' or alter 'the new roof affects the amount of water leaking into the attic' to 'the new roof reduces the amount of water leaking into the attic'.

Beware of ambiguous words

There are words whose meaning is obvious when you speak because of the inflection you use, but which are liable to misinterpretation on paper. Let me give you an example: 'I was a little concerned about last month's figures'. Try saying it. You can make it sound as if you were just mildly concerned, or as if you were really quite worried.

This is not a problem when you're speaking. But it is a problem when you're writing – how does the reader know which you mean? What's more, they probably won't think about it. They'll read it one way and never notice that you might have meant something else. This is another one of those times when you need that honest colleague or friend to read through your draft for you. Here are some more words which can fall into the same category, so keep a look out for them.

- quite
- fairly
- worried

Avoid tautology and redundant words

Never include words in your writing which serve no useful purpose. Tautology is the use of two or more words which mean the same and therefore unnecessarily repeat the same idea, such as 'combine together', which simply means combine, of course. Or 'erode away' where 'erode' would suffice.

We've touched on certain groups of redundant words already, such as some legal words, and many stock phrases. There are plenty more where they came from, such as the phrase 'at a later date' to mean later, and 'in order to' where simply 'to' would do: 'She kicked the door (in order) to open it'.

EXERCISE

Rewrite each of the sentences below without the redundant words or tautologies.

1 You must need a very small scalpel in order to bisect the plankton in two.

2 Please accept our thanks for assembling such a huge crowd together to hear the talk on the past history of our neolithic ancestors.

3 Please be advised that the two round glass globes you sent us seem to be filled to capacity with sawdust.

RESPONSE

Each sentence is printed with the redundant and tautologous words in italic type.

1 You must need a very small scalpel *in order* to bisect the plankton *in two*.

2 *Please accept our* thanks for assembling such a huge crowd *together* to hear the talk on the *past* history of our neolithic ancestors.

3 *Please be advised that* the two *round* glass globes you sent us seem to be filled *to capacity* with sawdust.

Use concrete rather than abstract nouns

'Transportation' is an abstract noun; 'car' is a concrete noun. The reason for avoiding abstract nouns is that they're more difficult to read:

- they're often longer
- they don't give the reader a clear visual picture
- a lot of them are very non-specific (such as situation, activities, operations).

Occasionally you have to use these words, but you should keep them to a minimum. It's far better to be more specific, edit the words out or replace them with verbs:

'The operation of this bulldozer is not easy' becomes 'This bulldozer isn't easy to operate.'

'When you take into consideration . . .' becomes 'When you consider . . .'.

'Acid rain accounts for the destruction of ancient stonework' becomes 'Acid rain destroys ancient stonework'.

Use active rather than passive verbs

'I was trampled by the elephant' uses a passive verb – the subject of the sentence is 'I' but I didn't actively do anything myself; something was done to me. In order to make a passive verb active, you usually have to change the subject of the sentence to whoever was responsible for the doing. In this case the elephant: 'The elephant trampled me'. To make passive verbs active, ask yourself who did the action in question?

This makes the writing flow more smoothly and gives it a livelier, more dynamic feel. Instead of a report or proposal full of people and objects sitting back while things are done to them, you have a document full of action, where people, businesses, objects and everything else are motivated and doing things. Here are some examples:

'The budget will be met by the department' becomes 'The department will meet the budget'.

'The school is attended by over 300 children' becomes 'Over 300 children attend the school'.

'The aeroplane will be painted by a team of people wearing magnetic boots' becomes 'A team of people wearing magnetic boots will paint the aeroplane'.

As a general rule, it's a good idea to limit passive verbs to around one every four or five sentences at the most. It is difficult to remove them from your writing altogether because there are times when you will need to use them:

1 If you don't know the subject of the verb, or it's irrelevant: 'The house had been painted bright yellow.'

2 When you want to draw attention to the object rather than the subject of the verb: 'It was the red car that was squashed by the steamroller.'

3 When you want to be deliberately vague: 'An error was made with your deliver.'

99

EXERCISE

Read through the following sentences, and improve them using the points we've covered in this chapter.

1   It is of considerable importance to ensure that under no circumstances should anyone fail to deactivate the overhead luminescent function at its local activation point on their departure to their place of residence, most notably immediately preceding the two-day holiday period at the termination of the standard working week.

2   It may be of interest to note that the the velocity of travel of a considerable number of railway vehicle driving operatives has been monitored over a considerable period of time, most particularly with reference to the shade of colour of the transport vehicle in question. The aforesaid measurements were recorded by qualified engineering personnel ensuring throughout that the only variable factor within the parameters of the experimentation was the said shade of colour of the transport vehicle. The overall result of this monitoring exercise was to establish a correlation between the speed of movement of the vehicle and the colouration of its external bodywork. It was established that the driving operatives displayed a tendency to accelerate their railway vehicles to a faster speed rating when operating a vehicle with red external bodywork than any other shade; conversely the lowest rates of celerity were recorded when monitoring vehicles whose bodywork was blue in colour.

3   Taking into consideration all the possible factors, there is clearly a dilemma here between the two opposing potential situations, that of existence and that of non-existence, leading to an ultimate and possibly irreversible decision.

RESPONSE

As usual, there's more than one right answer. Just make sure that you've spotted all the worst mistakes and come up with a brief, readable version.

1 *Always turn the lights out when you go home, especially on a Friday.*

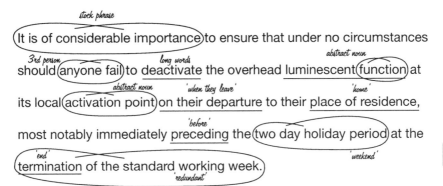

It is of considerable importance to ensure that under no circumstances should anyone fail to deactivate the overhead luminescent function at its local activation point on their departure to their place of residence, most notably immediately preceding the two day holiday period at the termination of the standard working week.

stock phrase *3rd person* *long words* *abstract noun* *abstract noun* *'when they leave'* *'home'* *'before'* *'end'* *'weekend'* *'redundant'*

101

2 *Thorough and controlled tests have shown that train drivers go fastest when they're driving red trains, and slowest when they're driving blue trains.*

It may be of interest to note that the velocity of travel of a considerable number of railway vehicle driving operatives has been monitored over a considerable period of time, most particularly with reference to the shade of colour of the transport vehicle in question. The aforesaid measurements were recorded by qualified engineering personnel ensuring throughout that the only variable factor within the

redundant *'speed'* *how many?* *'train'* *'drivers'* *stock phrase* *tautology* *'train'* *legalistic* *passive verb* *'engineers'* *'difference'*

abstract noun *legalistic* *tautology*

parameters of the experimentation was the (said) shade of colour of

'train' *redundant*

the (transport vehicle.) The overall result of this ~~monitoring exercise~~

redundant

was to establish a correlation between the speed ~~of movement~~ of the

abstract noun *redundant* *'we found ...'*

vehicle and the (colouration) of its external bodywork; it was

'drivers'

established that the (driving operatives) displayed a tendency to

'trains' *redundant*

accelerate their railway vehicles to a faster speed ~~rating~~ when

redundant

operating a vehicle with red external bodywork than any other shade;

'speeds' *passive*

conversely the lowest rates of celerity (were recorded) when monitoring

tautology

vehicles whose bodywork was blue (in colour.)

102

3   *To be or not to be; that is the question.*

Redundant/stock phrase

Taking into consideration all the possible factors, there is clearly a

abstract noun

dilemma here between the two opposing (potential situations,) that of

abstract noun *abstract noun*

(existence) and that of (non-existence,) leading to an ultimate and

possibly irreversible decision.

Summary

1 *General approach*

- match the style to the reader
- use everyday English
- be politically correct
- explain new ideas clearly.

2 *Phrasing and sentences*

- avoid jargon
- avoid stock phrases
- avoid clichés
- keep sentences and paragraphs short.

3 *Words*

- use short words
- avoid legal words and pomposity
- avoid neutral words
- beware of ambiguous words
- avoid tautology and redundant words
- use concrete rather than abstract nouns
- use active rather than passive verbs.

8
∎ ∎ ∎

Using plain English II: Mechanics

People will judge your professionalism on your ability to spell, punctuate and use the right word in the right place. You might feel that whether or not your reader accepts your proposal should depend entirely on the merit of your recommendation. Perhaps it should – but it won't.

If your readers can recognise good grammar, punctuation and the rest of it, you will vastly increase your chances of getting the result you want from your report or proposal if you follow the rules.

In the last chapter we discussed your writing style. There's good and bad style, but no right and wrong – there are degrees. You can write with poor style, quite reasonable style, very good style. When it comes to mechanics, it's black and white. If you spell examination with two 'x's it is wrong. It's not wrongish, or OK but not as good as if you'd left one of the 'x's out – it's just plain wrong.

This chapter is about the rules:

- **Vocabulary**

- **Spelling**

- **Abbreviations**

- **Punctuation**

In case you don't like rules very much, you'll find a section at the end of the chapter on rules you're allowed to break.

Vocabulary
■ ■ ■

We've already looked at the choice of words in terms of style in the last chapter – it's also important to use the correct word for what you're trying to say. How often have you read or heard someone say: 'The single most important criteria when choosing a car . . .'? In fact, of course, criteria is the plural. If there's only one of them, it's a criterion.

Unfortunately, there's no simple guideline to follow to make sure you always use these words correctly. The important thing is to understand that if your readers know the difference, they won't be impressed if you get it wrong. So, if in doubt, check it in a dictionary.

EXERCISE

It's impossible to give you a comprehensive list of frequently misused words, but here are 16 of the most common examples. See how many of the pairs you know the correct usage for (a score above 12 is good).

affect	effect
adverse	averse
principle	principal
stationery	stationary
illicit	elicit
inquire	enquire
flaunt	flout
allusion	illusion

complement	compliment
council	counsel
dependent	dependant
ensure	insure
disk	disc
mitigate	militate
practice	practise
advice	advise

RESPONSE

affect – verb meaning to influence: it affected me deeply

effect – noun meaning result or verb meaning to bring about: it had a deep effect on me/the new law will effect change in the country

adverse – adjective meaning unfavourable: it had an adverse effect on me

averse – adjective meaning opposed or disinclined: I am averse to powdered eggs (formerly 'averse from')

principle – noun meaning a standard or rule of conduct: it's against my principles to do that

principal – adjective or noun meaning most important: the principal rule, the principal of the school

stationery – noun meaning writing materials: I'm running out of stationery

stationary – adjective meaning not moving: that is a stationary vehicle

illicit – adjective meaning illegal: they were smuggling illicit goods into the country

elicit – verb meaning to give rise to: the question elicited a sharp response *inquire (inquiry)* – verb meaning to make an investigation : the police launched an immediate inquiry

enquire (enquiry) – verb meaning to ask: he enquired after her health

flaunt – verb meaning show off: she flaunted her new 24 carat gold earrings

flout – verb meaning to show contempt: They flouted the rules disgracefully

allusion – noun meaning a passing reference: were you making an allusion to my mother?

illusion – noun meaning a false impression of reality: he gave the illusion of being wealthy

complement – noun meaning something that completes, or verb meaning to make complete: one more member of the committee would give us a full complement, the scarf complements her dress

Compliment – noun meaning praise or verb meaning to praise: she complimented me on paying her such a kind compliment

109

council – noun meaning an assembly of people: the council meets every month

counsel – verb meaning to recommend or noun meaning recommendation: I counselled her to accept my counsel

dependent – adjective meaning reliant: I'm dependent on my job for my income

dependant – noun meaning a person who depends: he has three elderly dependants

ensure – verb meaning to make certain: I want to ensure that the water's not too hot before I get in the bath

insure – verb meaning to protect against risk: I have insured my car against being damaged by circus animals

disk – noun meaning a computer information storage device

disc – noun meaning a flat circular object

mitigate – verb meaning to moderate: the circumstances went some way to mitigate the blame attached to them

militate – verb meaning to influence (usually 'against' or 'for'): the evidence militated against their release

practice – noun: I'm going to put my ideas into practice

practise – verb: I'm going to practise the double bass until I'm an expert

advice – noun meaning recommendation: let me give you some advice . . .

advise – verb meaning to counsel: I advise you to think twice before you do that

---

As far as the last two examples are concerned, there are two other commonly misspelt words which follow the same rule: device/devise and licence/license. Again, the version which ends 'ce' is the noun; if it ends 'se' it's the verb.

Spelling
■ ■ ■

Again, if you misspell words which your reader can spell correctly, it gives a less professional impression. If you're in any doubt, look them up in a dictionary. Computer spell checkers are a mixed blessing. On the one hand, they can certainly pick up wrongly spelt or typed words which you might have missed. On the other hand, they tend to create a feeling of false confidence; they lead you to assume that once they've done their job the document is rendered error-free. It ain't necessarily so. If you mistype a word in any way which leaves it as another word, instead of as gobbledeygook, the spell check won't pick it up. So if you try to type 'and' but accidentally miss off the 'd', the spell check will think you've typed 'an' – which is of course a word – and allow it to pass. The same is true of their/there, too/to, off/of and many other common short words. So by all means use spell checkers, but don't rely on them.

Unfortunately, English is not an easy language to spell in – too much of it is irregular, and many spellings are impossible to deduce from the sound of the word. There are a few general rules and points worth making however:

■ The Americans tend to end words -ize which we end -ise (organise, rationalise, subsidise). If you want to use the English form, or you think your readers would prefer it, use the -ise ending.

■ A similar rule applies to the 'u' in words such as colour, favour, humour; the English version retains the 'u'; the Americans drop it to give: color, favor, humor.

■ Why does targeted have one 't' in the middle and regretted have two? There's a rule you can follow here: If the stress falls on the final syllable of the word (reg*ret*), you double the final letter when you add -ed. If it falls on an earlier syllable (*tar*get) you retain the single letter at the end. Other examples of retaining the single letter include marketed, offered, focused, benefited. A final 'l', however is always doubled, as in travelled.

■ If you are turning an adjective ending in a single or double 'l' (magical, full, special, dull) into an adverb, you always end up with a double 'll' in the middle: magically, fully, specially, dully.

■ The rule 'i before e except after c' is worth remembering. The exceptions are, or can be:

   a words in which the 'ei' is *not* pronounced 'ee' (such as heinous or inveigle)

   b the word seize

   c some personal and place names.

111

Commonly misspelt words

Again, this can't be comprehensive, but look through this list and make sure that if you can't confidently spell any of the words in it, you can trust yourself to look them up in a dictionary rather than guess:

accommodate	embarrass	high-flier
appal	enroll	mileage
battalion	fulfil	parallel
commemorate	gauge	privilege
commitment	harass	questionnaire

Abbreviations

■ ■ ■

Try to avoid abbreviating words out of laziness, such as approx. for approximately; it implies the reader isn't worth bothering to write it out in full for. (In the case of approximately, you can usually replace it with 'about' which is briefer and easier to read.)

However, when it comes to shortening long titles to their initials, such as EC for European Community, this can only be a good thing. It makes the text far easier to read, and saves boring repetition of long names and titles. The drawback is that a lot of these abbreviations are meaningless while the full title, although lengthy, does explain what the company, organisation or association does.

There is a simple rule for overcoming this problem: if you only mention the organisation once, use its full name. If you mention it more than once, use the full version the first time immediately followed by the abbreviation in brackets. For example 'the Local Education Authority (LEA) . . .'. After that, simply refer to it as the LEA or, for variation, the authority.

Punctuation
■ ■ ■

Capital letters

Capital letters are harder to read than lower case letters. As children, we learn them last and use them less. So it's better when we're writing to use them only where it would be incorrect not to. Apart from the beginning of sentences, and proper names, the other times when you have to use them are:

113

- Organisations, companies, ministries and places (House of Commons or Westminster Abbey)
- Acts of parliament (the Act of Union)
- Any label formed from a proper name (Marxist, Thatcherite)
- Countries; capitalise North, South, East and West if they form part of the name of the country (South Africa) but not otherwise
- Titles when used with the name, but not otherwise (President Johnson but the president, the Duke of York but the duke)
- Some periods of history (Black Death, Renaissance)
- God

English being the perverse language it is, there are of course exceptions to the rule. But these are the chief categories which need capitals – it's a guide, not an exhaustive list; *The Economist Style Guide* gives a much fuller list (details at the end of this chapter). Avoid using any other capitals; for example, you don't need to capitalise government, ministry (when you're not giving its title), production manager – or even managing director. If you refer to the local council by its full title, such as Warwickshire County Council, you'll need to capitalise it. But if you subsequently call it the council, you can drop the capital 'C'.

Apostrophes

The apostrophe is probably the most frequently misused piece of punctuation in the English language. People most commonly misuse it when they want to make a word plural, for example:

Pick your own tomatoe's.

Back in the 1880's . . .

All the department's were represented.

All these examples are wrong, for a very good reason – you don't need an apostrophe anywhere to pluralise a word. That isn't what apostrophes were invented for. They actually have two purposes:

1 to show possession

2 to show that a letter has been missed out.

The possessive

Add an 's' to the person, people or thing doing the possessing: the children's shoes, the tree's shade, the snake's eyes. The apostrophe goes after whoever is possessing, so in the last example, if you were talking about the eyes of lots of snakes the apostrophe would go after the final 's' of snakes: the snakes' eyes.

A good way to remember it is to say to yourself 'the .... *belonging to* the ....'

■ If they're the eyes belonging to the snake (singular) you would write: the snake's eyes.

■ If they're the eyes belonging to the snakes (plural) you would write: the snakes' eyes.

If the person or people (or snakes) doing the possessing already have an 's' on the end, you don't add another one; simply stick the apostrophe on the end – that's why you've never seen anyone write 'the snakes's eyes'. The only times when you would add an 's' after a singular word that ends in 's' are:

■ if it's a proper name (Mr Jones's, St James's)

■ if the word ends in a double 'ss' (the boss's).

You never use an apostrophe with a possessive pronoun (a word indicating possession which replaces a noun). These are words like: yours, hers, its, theirs, ours.

115

Missing letters

You also use an apostrophe to show that one or more letters have been left out, as in: isn't, shouldn't (both missing the 'o' of 'not'), what's (meaning 'what is' or 'what has'), can't (for cannot) and so on.

It's and its

A lot of people find these two words very confusing; 'its' is a possessive pronoun and therefore has no apostrophe, while 'it's' is short for 'it is' and does have one. The easiest way to tell each time you write the word is to say it in your head as 'it is'. If it makes sense, it's short for it is and has an apostrophe. Otherwise it doesn't. For example, 'I gave the dog its breakfast.' Try the technique: 'I gave the dog it is breakfast.' Complete nonsense. It clearly isn't short for it is, so it shouldn't have anapostrophe.Here's another example: 'Its a great day to go pot-holing.' Try the technique: 'It is a great day to go pot-holing.' That makes sense – it's short for 'it is' so it *does* have an apostrophe, in place of the missing 'i'.

EXERCISE

Correct the following sentences, removing or inserting apostrophes as necessary.

1 The departments help wasnt exactly what I wanted, but the result's were better than I'd expected.

2 The lions excitement showed in it's face.

3 'Its not yours, its ours' we shouted as the childrens' footsteps disappeared.

RESPONSE

1 The department's help wasn't exactly what I wanted, but the results were better than I'd expected.

2 The lion's excitement showed in its face.

3 'It's not yours, it's ours' we shouted as the children's footsteps disappeared.

Commas

Fashions in commas change. But the trend is towards using fewer commas than used to be considered proper. There are two reasons for using a comma nowadays:

1 Where the sentence would be unclear without it either because the sense would be confusing or because the sentence would be too long. For example: 'I decided on an alteration of course'. I'll repeat that with a comma and you can see what I mean: 'I decided on an alteration, of course'. Here's another example. Version one: 'I removed   20 commas which made the article harder to read.' Version two: "I removed 20 commas, which made the article harder to read.'

2 To show where you've inserted a phrase or clause, for instance: 'The cat, whose favourite food was fresh fish, finished off the plateful.' If you removed the part of the sentence between the commas, the remainder would still make sense.

117

Colons

The main reason for using a colon is to signpost the next piece of text (as in 'for example:'). It is often used in this way to introduce a complete list. For example:

Several departments contributed to this report: production, marketing, accounts, distribution and personnel.

Don't use a colon, however, if the list is incomplete. It's better to use words like 'such as', 'including' or 'like', in which case you shouldn't use the colon at all:

Several departments contributed to this report, including production, distribution and accounts.

Semi-colons

These have two functions. Firstly, you can use them when you feel as if you want more than a comma and less than a full stop; it can happen more often than you might think. Secondly, you can use them to break up lists which already contain commas. Commas are the best way to break up lists:

'government departments such as defence, transport, health and the environment.'

But if the items in the list already have commas in them, this can become very confusing for the reader. When that happens use semi-colons:

'government departments such as health; education; agriculture, food and fisheries; the foreign office and employment.'

Hyphens

Hyphens, like commas, are chiefly there for clarity. The more there are the harder it becomes to read the text. Check your dictionary if you think a word might be hyphenated but if in doubt, don't use a hyphen unless the meaning is unclear without it. When you do use them, don't leave a space bar either side – as you would for parentheses – as this is misleading and difficult to read.

Exclamation marks

Only use these for exclamations, never to tell the reader the sentence was supposed to be funny.

Rules you can break

■ ■ ■

There are certain grammatical rules which used to be fashionable but which are no longer considered so important. Of course, bearing in mind the point in the last chapter about matching your style to your readers, you'll find that the more old-fashioned reader may still be resistant to these changes of use. But for most purposes, you can now feel free to break the following 'rules'.

Never start a sentence with 'and', 'but' or 'because'

William Blake clearly wasn't too bothered by grammatical convention when he wrote 'And did those feet, in ancient times . . .'.

119

Not only can you start a sentence with these words, you can start paragraphs with them too. They can be very useful for this purpose, as they tend to add emphasis to what you are about to say.

Never finish a sentence with a preposition

This was often quite hard to obey. Prepositions are all those little words that aren't anything else, like up, of, to, in and so on. There are times when the only way to avoid putting one of them at the end of a sentence involves twisting the sentence so self-consciously that it becomes even harder to follow.

There is a story (no doubt apocryphal) about Winston Churchill's view of this rule. His secretary told him he should rephrase a sentence because he had finished it with a preposition, and he supposedly replied: 'There are some things up with which I will not put!'

Never split an infinitive

Apart from anything else, I would estimate the proportion of the present population that can honestly identify a split infinitive every time without error to be well below 5 per cent. It seems a little pointless to worry ourselves unduly about something that most people can't recognise. Furthermore, according to *Fowler's Modern English Usage* a lot of people who object to splitting infinitives can't actually identify them correctly. So even if we kept our infinitives beautifully together, we should still upset this group who would think we were splitting them when we weren't.

For the record, I'll briefly explain what a split infinitive is. A present tense infinitive is made up of 'to' plus the verb, as in 'to help', 'to hear', 'to understand', 'to be'. If you put any word between these two you are splitting the infinitive: 'to clearly understand' or 'to suddenly hear'. The best known modern example of a split infinitive is in the title sequence of Star Trek where the voice over says '. . . to boldly go where no man has gone before'.

The usage that Fowler says most people misunderstand is this: 'to be really happy' is not a split infinitive, although some people think it is. The infinitive in the phrase is 'to be', so the split version would be 'to really be happy'.

Never use the same word twice

According to this rule, Hamlet should never have said 'Words, words, words.' The idea is that if you repeat a noun or verb, you should find a different word for it each time. So if you're writing about your house, you have to call it your residence next time you mention it, then your home, your domicile and so on. Normally the effect is simply to confuse the reader – then baffle them, confound them, bewilder them, leave them nonplussed and so on.

Of course, sometimes an alternative word can add variety;

you can use your common sense. But don't feel obliged to follow this rule blindly, just for the sake of it.

Your reference library
■ ■ ■

There are certain reference books which no-one who has to write reports and proposals should be without. Keep them near your desk, and refer to them as frequently as you like.

The Complete Plain Words *by Sir Ernest Gowers*

I'm sure that if I were being entirely objective I would have to list a dictionary and a thesaurus above this book in importance. However, since I recommend all three as the very minimum that any writer's library should contain, I don't consider that I need to list them in order of usefulness. I'm putting this book first because it's a good read. It has also been, for the last 45 years, the definitive work on how to write plain, clear English.

Dictionary

If you don't have a dictionary, buy the most comprehensive one you can afford, and expect to have to replace it every few years; not only do new words get added, but some words change their usage.

Thesaurus

A dictionary isn't much use if you can't remember the word you're trying to think of – what are you going to look it up under? What you need is a thesaurus – the best known is Roget's Thesaurus – which contains lists of synonyms (groups of words with the same, or very similar, meaning).

Fowler's Modern English Usage *(Oxford University Press)*

If you are going to have more than these three basic books, buy a copy of *Fowler's Modern English Usage*. It will answer just about any question of grammar or syntax you can devise, explain the difference between metaphors and similes, and tell you all about punctuation, plurals, subjunctives, participles – and split infinitives.

The Economist Style Guide *(The Economist Books Ltd)*

This guide to English usage is the one *The Economist* gives to its journalists. If you follow all its guidelines your reports and proposals will read like *Economist* articles – you could do worse.

The Penguin Dictionary of Troublesome Words *(Penguin)*

The title speaks for itself. If you can't remember how many 'r's in embarrass, or whether you compare things *with* each other or *to* each other, get a copy of this book.

It's difficult to exaggerate the value of a small but good reference shelf like this. And if you're at all unsure of your writing skills it will help you turn out high quality writing. And don't worry if you think you're hopeless at writing clearly and following all the guidelines: English is a sod of a language, and we all look things up from time to time.

SUMMARY

Check:

- your choice of words
- spelling
- abbreviations.

Punctuation:

- capital letters
- apostrophes
- commas
- colons
- semi-colons.

123

Build up a small library of reference books.

9
■ ■ ■

Making it look readable

The way a report or proposal looks is the first chance the reader has to judge it. And we all know about first impressions. The more approachable it is the more likely the recipient is to read and understand it – which is of course the aim.

This chapter is about the features which make a report or proposal more readable, and how to use them. These include:

■ Layout

■ Appendices

■ The use of charts and graphs.

Layout
■　■　■

The visual appearance of your proposal or report is vital. An easily readable document gives the impression of being more organised than an unapproachable one. As a general rule, in fact, it *is* more organised. It's hard to make the information appear well-ordered when it's not, and it's quite hard to present a document really badly when you've thought it out clearly.

Of course, the fact that your proposal or report looks organised will convey the message to your readers that *you* are well organised. In fact, they will most likely attribute to you personally all the qualities they associate with your proposal or report: organised, professional, clear-thinking and authoritative. So the work you put into laying out your material approachably is an investment in more than just the document itself – you're building your own reputation at the same time.

Let's have a look at the techniques you can use to make your proposal or report look more readable:

Spacing

It stands to reason that the wider the spacing the less text the reader has to take in on each page. So double space your text.

Margins

Leave wide margins; again so there's lots of 'white space' on the page. This also has the effect of focusing attention on the text, giving the appearance of being more important. Ideally, the right hand margin should be unjustified (in other words the right hand ends of every line of text should not line up); this makes the document look friendlier and more approachable. There are times, however, when you will need to justify the right hand margin:

- When you are producing a document that needs to look very straight and formal.

- If the page is at risk of looking confusing because it has a lot of diagrams, illustrations and so on. In this case, you may find that justifying the right hand margin has the effect of 'tidying up' the page; obviously if you do this you must be consistent throughout the document.

127

Headings

Not only do headings break up the page and improve the layout of the document, they also tell the reader what the next section is about. It may be a part of the subject they're not so interested in and the heading tells them that they can skip through it. For this reason, you should never be tempted to be clever with headings at the expense of clarity. If you're on a road you've never driven on before trying to get to London, you don't want witty signposts saying 'Capital Destination!' You want signs that say 'London'.

For the same reason you should use sub-headings whenever it could be useful. Not only do they help in the same way as headings, they are also particularly handy for the reader if they want to look back through the document and find that bit about whatever-it-was.

Sections

It's a good idea in a long or complicated document to summarise each section briefly, to help the reader scan it or remember it quickly if they refer back to it later. For example:

'So those are the four options we seem to have:

- leave the building alone for the time being

- try to redesign it in a form in which we can use it

- pull the whole structure down and rebuild it

- try to sell it to an organisation that it would be better suited to; i.e. one that never needs to fit anything more than 18 inches wide through any of the doors.'

128 *Numbering sections*

These can also add to the clarity if the sequence is logical; if you use too many numbers, however, you can start to confuse the reader. You can:

- Number each paragraph separately in sequence; if you do this you will improve the readability of the proposal or report if you also use headings and sub-headings.

- Give each headed section a number ('4. Potential drawbacks').

- Give each headed section a number and number the paragraphs within it: 4.1, 4.2, 4.3 and so on. (Any further subdivision, as in 2.1.1, 2.1.2, 2.1.3, tends to become confusing and is better avoided.)

Paragraphs

Every time you begin a fresh thought, begin a fresh paragraph. Ideally a paragraph should contain between two and four sentences; certainly you get the best visual effect if it is wider than it is deep once it's printed on the page. Leave a double line space between paragraphs to help keep the document looking approachable.

Lists

One of the best ways to present complex information is in list form. Normally you need an introductory line or two explaining what you're listing, and then the information itself. Here's an example, which also gives you a few ideas for devices you can use to pick out the things you're listing:

- bullet points
- square points
- dashes
- numbers
- relevant icons (if you have them on your word processor); for example you could start each point with an icon of an aeroplane if you were listing the four best sites to build a new runway for the local city airport. Don't get too silly though – it will distract from what you're saying.

Of course, you may work for an organisation that has its own house style for reports. This may well follow the guidelines above but if not, take advantage of any opportunity to adapt the rules. If possible, see if you can get the house style revised. You could even offer to put forward a proposal for revising it – and show them how it should be done.

One other point. If your proposals and reports are typed on a word processor, don't try to 'design' them. If you use four different fonts to a page it will look a mess. Be consistent; for example all main headings are centred in capitals, all subheadings are on the left in bold, or whatever. Only use one font, or possibly a second for headlines only. One useful feature of some programmes is being able to put things in boxes. Used sparingly, this can help to present information clearly.

The proof of the pudding

In case you are at all sceptical about the benefits of clear layout, or would like proof of the difference it makes, you'll find opposite the text of the first part of this chapter. It is quite unaltered apart from the layout (and concomitant changes such as removing headings and sub-headings). Look back at the last couple of pages as well, and decide which version you'd prefer to read.

Let's have a look at the techniques you can use to make your proposal or report look more readable. It stands to reason that the wider the spacing the less text the reader has to take in on each page. So double space your text. Leave wide margins; again so there's lots of 'white space' on the page. This also has the effect of focusing attention on the text, giving the appearance of being more important. Ideally, the right hand margin should be unjustified (in other words the right hand ends of every line of text should not line up); this makes the document look friendlier and more approachable. There are times, however, when you will need to justify the right hand margin, either when you are producing a document that needs to look very straight and formal, or if the page is at risk of looking confusing because it has a lot of diagrams, illustrations and so on. In this case, you may find that justifying the right hand margin has the effect of 'tidying up' the page; obviously if you do this you must be consistent throughout the document.

Not only do headings break up the page and improve the layout of the document; they also tell the reader what the next section is about. It may be a part of the subject they're not so interested in and the heading tells them that they can skip through it. For this reason, you should never be tempted to be clever with headings at the expense of clarity. If you're on a road you've never driven on before trying to get to London, you don't want witty signposts saying 'Capital Destination!' You want signs that say 'London'. For the same reason you should use sub-headings whenever it could be useful. Not only do they help in the same way as headings, they are also particularly handy for the reader if they want to look back through the document and find that bit about whatever-it-was. It's a good idea in a long or complicated document to summarise each section briefly, to help the reader scan it or remember it quickly if they refer back to it later. For example: 'So those are the four options we seem to have: leave the building alone for the time being; try to redesign it in a form in which we can use it; pull the whole structure down and rebuild it; try to sell it to an organisation that it would be better suited to; i.e. one that never needs to fit anything more than 18" wide through any of the doors.'

Numbered sections can also add to the clarity if the sequence is logical; if you use too many numbers, however, you can start to confuse the reader. You can number each paragraph separately in sequence; if you do this you will improve the readability of the proposal or report if you also use headings and sub-headings. Or you could give each headed section a number ('4. Potential drawbacks'), or give each headed section a number and number the paragraphs within it: 4.1, 4.2, 4.3 and so on. (Any further subdivision, as in 2.1.1, 2.1.2, 2.1.3, tends to become confusing and is better avoided.) Every time you begin a fresh thought, begin a fresh paragraph Ideally a paragraph should contain between two and four sentences; certainly you get the best visual effect if it is wider than it is deep once it's printed on the page. Leave a double line space between paragraphs to help keep the document looking approachable.

One of the best ways to present complex information is in list form. Normally you need an introductory line or two explaining what you're listing, and then the information itself. Here are a few ideas for devices you can use to pick out the things you're listing: bullet points, square points, dashes, numbers, relevant icons (if you have them on your word processor); for example you could start each point with an icon of an aeroplane if you were listing the four best sites to build a new runway for the local city airport. Don't get too silly though – it will distract from what you're saying.

EXERCISE

Now it's your turn to try it. Work out how you would rearrange the following block of text, with minimal changes to the words (other than adding headings and sub-headings), to make it look more readable.

There are several different ways of making coffee, and most people are very fussy about the one they prefer. For a start there's instant coffee; it's certainly the quickest method and a lot of people genuinely prefer the taste. For those who like their coffee made with all milk, it's easy to do this with instant coffee. It's also very easy to make for one person, without any wastage. On the other hand, it's arguably the least healthy and some of the varieties taste extremely unpleasant. Then there's filter coffee. You can make this in a machine, which takes a little while, and isn't very hot when it comes out. But it has the benefit that you can leave it on a hotplate for some time and go back later for a second cup. And you can make enough for several people at once. You can also make filter coffee in a cafetière. This is usually only enough for a few people. It isn't terribly hot because it has to be left to stand for a short while, but it's hotter than filter coffee made in a machine. One other variety of coffee which is increasing in popularity is espresso coffee. You need an espresso machine to make this in; it works by forcing steam through the coffee grounds; the steam then condenses into coffee. Espresso coffee is usually very hot and very strong. It is commonly considered to make the best black coffee, and when combined with milk it is rich and strong. The two biggest disadvantages are the fact that the machines are not very big. You can make several small cups of strong black coffee (Mediterranean style) from them, but only a couple of mugs worth. The other disadvantage is that the machines are a hassle to wash up if you don't have a dishwasher.

RESPONSE

As usual, there's no exact correct answer. But your version should look something like this.

COFFEE MAKING

There are several different ways of making coffee, and most people are very fussy about the one they prefer.

Instant coffee

Advantages

- It's certainly the quickest method and a lot of people genuinely prefer the taste.

- For those who like their coffee made with all milk, it's easy to do this with instant coffee.

- It's also very easy to make for one person, without any wastage.

Disadvantages

- It's arguably the least healthy and some of the varieties taste extremely unpleasant.

Filter coffee – machine

Advantages

- This has the benefit that you can leave it on a hotplate for some time and go back later for a second cup.

- And you can make enough for several people at once.

Disadvantages

- This takes a little while.

- It isn't very hot when it comes out.

134

Filter coffee – cafetière

Advantages

■ It's hotter than filter coffee made in a machine.

Disadvantages

■ This is usually only enough for a few people.
■ It isn't terribly hot because it has to be left to stand for a short while.

Espresso coffee

One other variety of coffee which is increasing in popularity is espresso coffee. You need an espresso machine to make this in; it works by forcing steam through the coffee grounds; the steam then condenses into coffee.

Advantages

■ Espresso coffee is usually very hot.

■ It is commonly considered to make the best black coffee, and when combined with milk it is rich and strong.

Disadvantages

■ The machines are not very big. You can make several small cups of strong black coffee (Mediterranean style) from them, but only a couple of mugs worth.

■ The machines are a hassle to wash up if you don't have a dishwasher.

135

Appendices

■   ■   ■

We've already discussed the importance of including hard facts in your proposal or report, and backing up your assertions with supporting data. However, you don't necessarily need to include this in the main body of the report. The shorter the bulk of the report is, the less your readers will wince when it lands on their desk. So certainly include all the important information in the text, but move the supporting data to the appendices.

Technical information in particular is often better supplied in an appendix; statistics, equations, graphs and sets of figures often don't need to be in the main document at all. You can always include a summary within the text with a reference to the fact that the full figures are in Appendix 3. Always make sure that you refer the reader clearly to any further information.

One other valuable use of appendices is when certain information is likely to be updated later. In this case, putting it in an appendix makes it easy to swop with the newer data when the time comes.

Don't include appendices for the sake of it. The shorter your report, the happier most of your readers will be. Of course you should include all the information they might genuinely want, but don't be tempted to add extra to show how much work you've put in. Your readers want quality, not quantity. If possible, they specifically want quality *without* quantity. Remember the Duke of Wellington's message to the War Office: 'I apologise for the length of these despatches but I did not have time to make them shorter.'

Using charts and graphs

■ ■ ■

The idea of a report or proposal is, of course, to give the reader all the information they want in the most helpful form for them to:

- ■ take it in as quickly as possible
- ■ follow it easily
- ■ understand it
- ■ remember it.

For a lot of information, the best way to achieve this is to present it in the form of graphs or charts. Whether you use them in an appendix or in the main body of the report they can give a degree of clarity to technical data, surveys, comparisons and so on that is difficult if not impossible to achieve without them.

137

Graphs and charts can be simple to produce and hugely informative to read – as long as you know how to use them. The important thing is to know which kind of chart to use when, so you're not left thinking 'Help! What do I need here? A bar chart? A pie chart? Columns? Dots? I don't know. How do I choose?' That's what the final part of this chapter is about.

The comparisons

It's really very easy; different types of charts have different uses. So you choose according to what it is you want to demonstrate – time comparison, correlation, different items and so on. You just need to learn what the key types of chart are and what you should use them to illustrate. All charts compare things to each other. So the most useful way to go about choosing the best kind of chart is to work out first what you are comparing.

Components

This is when you want to divide a single item or figure into its component parts, and demonstrate what percentage of the whole each component makes up. You might want to use fish living in the ornamental pond in reception as the 'whole', and show what percentage of them is gold, what percentage is black, what percentage white and what percentage blotchy. Or take last year's sales figures and show what proportion of them was contributed by each division.

If you want to demonstrate anything to do with share, or a percentage of the total, you're looking at a component comparison.

Items

Here, the performance of different items is being measured: How does the population of black fish compare with that of gold, white and blotchy fish? You're not concerned with the size of the total population as you were with the component comparison. How do our top four products rank in terms of total income earned since their launch?

If you want to show things as being larger or smaller than each other – or equal – you are making an item comparison.

Time series

The key word here is trend. If you want to show how things have increased, decreased, fluctuated or remained static over a time period, you are making a time series comparison. You may want to show how two or three things have changed; it's still a time series comparison.

You might be demonstrating how the population of black goldfish has changed over the last ten years. You don't want to focus the readers attention on what proportion of the fish are black, or how many are black rather than any other colour. Simply how the population of black goldfish changes. The monthly income of a particular branch over the last 12 months would be a time series comparison.

Frequency distribution

These comparisons divide the subject into increasing numerical ranges such as:

- under £100, £101–£300, £301– £500 etc.
- aged under 18, 18– 25, 26–35 etc.
- less than 1 month, 1–2 months, 2–3 months etc.

You then compare how many of the items in question fall into each section of the range. You might want to illustrate what percentage of the people who read your newspaper is under 18, what percentage is between 18 and 25 and so on.

139

Or you might be wondering about those blotchy goldfish. How blotchy are they? Are they basically white with less than 10 per cent of their scales black? Or more than 10 per cent black but less than 25 per cent? Frequency distributions tend to be about range, concentration and distribution.

Correlation

This concerns whether the relationship between two variable factors follows a pattern. Does the Managing Director's salary always go up in proportion to company profits? Are there always more gold goldfish in the years when there are fewer white fish? The important words here are vary with, in relation to, decrease with and so on.

The charts

So that's a summary of the main kinds of comparison you might want to make. Now let's look at the most common types of chart and see which kind of comparison to use each one for.

Pie chart

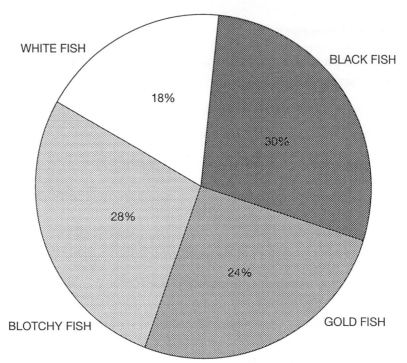

Proportion of goldfish of different colours

140

These charts compare components. Here are the most important things you need to know about pie charts:

- Allow yourself a maximum of six components, otherwise it becomes too confusing.

- The eye automatically reads a pie chart clockwise, starting at the 12 o'clock position. So if you want to emphasise one segment of it as being the most important, you should start this segment at 12 o'clock (and going clockwise). Shade the most important segment darkest (or the most striking colour if you are using colour).

- The most important section doesn't have to be the biggest.

- Stick to circles. If you compare the market share of five airlines that dominate a single route, and you do it by drawing five aeroplanes in different sizes, proportionate to the market share, you are using a form of pie chart. However, you will almost certainly confuse the reader because the eye can't take in the proportions so accurately when it has to interpret drawings of aeroplanes as it does when the information is presented in a simple circle. (This doesn't mean you can't explode your pie chart or make it 3D – it's OK to do that.)

- *Never* use two pie charts together to compare the components of two totals (percentage fish of each colour in two different ponds, for example). It makes the information very hard to extract. Use two 100 per cent bar charts or column charts (you'll find out what they are in just a moment).

141

Bar chart

Use a bar chart for item comparison or correlation. Bear the following points in mind:

Population size of different coloured goldfish

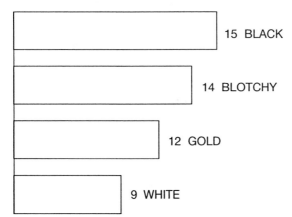

15 BLACK

14 BLOTCHY

12 GOLD

9 WHITE

Correlation between gold coloured and white coloured fish populations

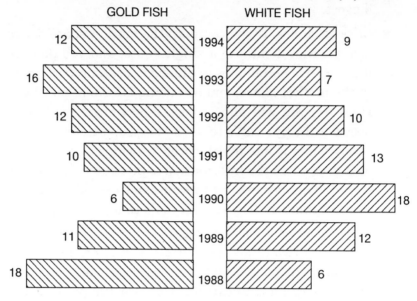

- Arrange the items on bar charts horizontally, not vertically. You can put the items in any order you like, according to what you want to emphasise. For example if you want to compare levels of income, you might want to put the items in order with the highest earning at the top, followed by the next highest and so on. But you could arrange them alphabetically if you preferred, or geographically. In fact, any way that seems appropriate.

- Always draw bar charts with bars that are wider than the spaces in between them.

- Write the numerical value at the end of each bar, or put a scale along the top. Don't do both. The numbers are more precise but the scale will give a better grasp of comparative size at a quick glance – decide which is more important for your readers.

- A 100 per cent bar chart shows you a component comparison in a bar instead of a pie shape. It's not as easy to interpret as a pie chart, but it's better if you're comparing two totals to each other:

100% Bar chart showing percentage fish
of each colour in consecutive years

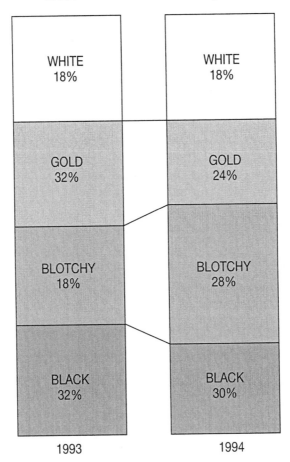

1993   1994

143

Column chart showing changes in population of black goldfish over 10 years

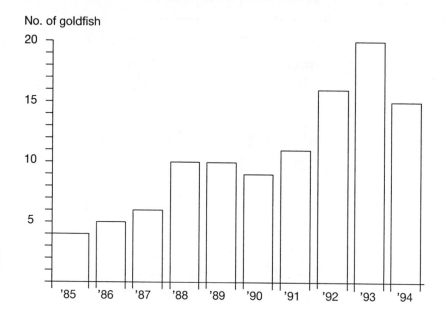

No. of goldfish

Chart showing frequency distribution of blotches

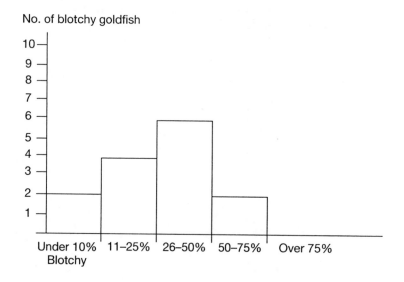

No. of blotchy goldfish

Use a column chart to make a time series comparison or a frequency distribution comparison. Remember the following points:

- Make the columns wider than the space between them.

- You can divide each column into shaded sections to show how, for example, each year's income was made up from the different regions.

- You can shade historical information in one colour, and continue the chart from the 'now' point onwards in a different colour to show projections.

- A step chart is a column chart without any spaces between the columns. It draws attention to the abrupt changes between the data being compared. If this is the aspect that you want to emphasise, use a step chart.

145

There are two reasons why column charts are less useful than bar charts for showing item comparisons:

1 They are likely to confuse readers because they expect to be reading a time series comparison, and it may take them a moment or two to realise that they're not.

2 Very simply – there's more room with a bar chart to label each bar.

Line chart

Changes in population of black goldfish over 10 years

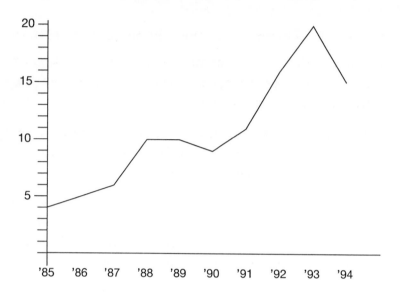

146

This is also used for time series comparisons. Here are the key points:

- This is often the easiest type of chart to draw and the clearest to read.

- Make sure the line which shows the trend is the strongest on the chart – stronger than the baseline.

- You can show more than one line on the chart; for example you could track the performance of your top three products over a time period. Putting all the lines on one chart allows you to compare them against each other. However, as usual, using too many lines can be horribly confusing. Try to limit yourself to two, or three at the outside.

- If you shade in the area below the line on the chart, you have created a surface chart. This gives you the option of comparing two or three lines on the same

Surface chart showing changes in black and blotchy fish populations over 10 years

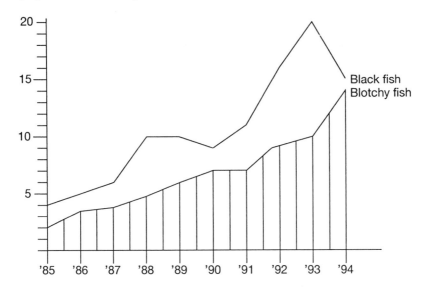

chart quite clearly. It doesn't really work, however, if they overlap.

There are two factors to consider when you're choosing between a column chart and a line chart for making a time series
comparison:

1 If you are marking only a few time points (say the monthly figures for the last six months) use a column chart. But if you have a lot (the monthly figures for the last five years, say) it's far clearer to use a line chart.

2 A column chart shows a clear divide between one column and the next, so it's good if you want to emphasise the distinction between, for example, each month's figures. A line chart is better for illustrating continuous development – it draws attention to the overall trend in monthly income.

Dot chart

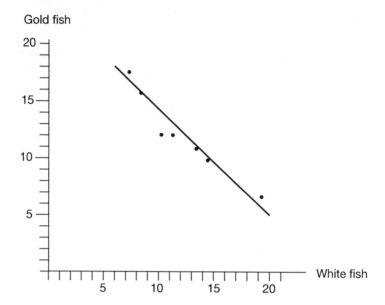

Demonstration that there is a correlation between gold fish and white fish populations

This is used for showing correlation. The key points to remember are:

- One of the two factors you're comparing runs along the *x* axis and the other is marked on the *y* axis.

- This kind of chart can be very helpful, but readers may not be used to interpreting them so explain them in the text or an extended caption.

- If there is a correlation the dots will be grouped in a line (where the value of *x* is high, the value of *y* is low, for example). If there is no correlation the dots will be scattered; this kind of chart is sometimes known as a scatter chart.

**How the graph looks when there is no correlation
between gold fish and white fish populations**

Gold fish

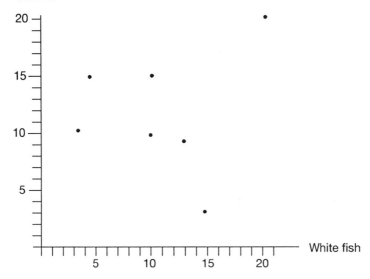

White fish

149

EXERCISE

Each of the following types of information can be represented in chart form. For each one decide what type of comparison it is, and which type of chart you would use to illustrate it.

1 How would you show the comparative shoe sizes of everyone in your immediate family?

Type of comparison:

Chart:

2 How fast do your customers pay their invoices? Show what proportion of them pay early, on time, late or very late.

Type of comparison:

Chart:

3 Show how the total contents of your fridge is made up, in terms of fresh food, frozen food, unopened food and mouldy food.

Type of comparison:

Chart:

4 What's the relationship, if any, between the length of time your customers have been buying from you, and the volume of their orders?

Type of comparison:

Chart:

5 How has your consumption of hard boiled eggs fluctuated over the past five years?

Type of comparison:

Chart:

6 What percentage of your employees are under 25, 25–40, 40–55 or over 55?

Type of comparison:

Chart:

RESPONSE

1 How would you show the comparative shoe sizes of everyone in your immediate family?

Type of comparison: Item

Chart: Bar chart

2 How fast do your customers pay their invoices? Show what proportion of them pay early, on time, late or very late.

Type of comparison: Frequency distribution

Chart: Column chart

3 Show how the total contents of your fridge is made up, in terms of fresh food, frozen food, unopened food and mouldy food.

Type of comparison: Component

Chart: Pie chart

4 What's the relationship, if any, between the length of time your customers have been buying from you, and the volume of their orders?

Type of comparison: Correlation

Chart: Bar chart or dot chart

5 How has your consumption of hard boiled eggs fluctuated over the past five years?

Type of comparison: Time series

Chart: Column chart or line chart

6 What percentage of your employees are under 25, 25–40, 40–55 or over 55?

Type of comparison: Frequency distribution

Chart: Column chart

NB: In case this one caught you out, it's not a component comparison, calling for a pie chart, because the emphasis is on the distribution, not the total number.

Flow charts

These are the other kind of chart which you might want to use, and which we haven't mentioned yet. They are invaluable for creating a common visual language that everyone understands. The trick, with any type of flow chart, is to keep it simple. There are three main types of flow chart which you might want to use in a proposal or report:

1 Work-flow chart

2 Schematic flow chart

3 Detailed flow chart.

Work-flow chart

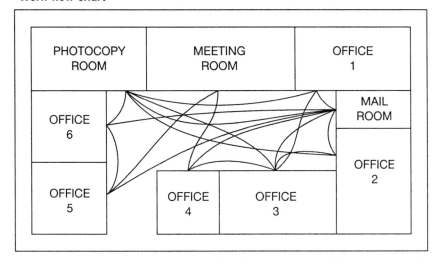

This is the best way to report on the way work physically moves around an office or factory. Make a representational floor plan and mark on it how the people, the paperwork or whatever you're concerned with, move around in the course of a day. For example, an order form may arrive at reception in the post and be passed to the sales office, then to the photo-copier, then one copy goes over to accounts and one down to distribution and so on. This kind of chart is useful for work efficiency reports, for one office or a whole building.

Schematic flow chart

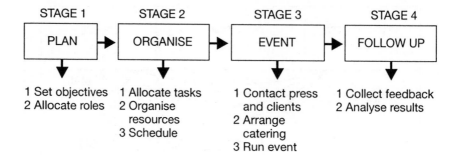

This gives a visual overview of the essential steps in a process or project, drawn chronologically from left to right. It can be very useful in proposals for demonstrating how work would be executed if the proposal were accepted.

Detailed flow chart

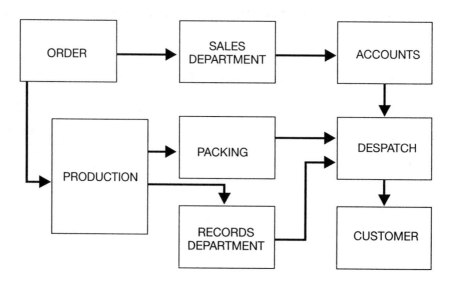

This is possibly the most misused flow chart there is. It can be tremendously helpful in explaining the flow of work from one function to the next – the danger is in putting in too much information. If you understand the process clearly yourself, it can be difficult to recognise when you've made it too complex for someone who's new to it. If in doubt, get someone else who doesn't know the process to take a look at the chart for you.

The golden rule for using charts is: the less information you include in them the easier they are to follow. Keep it simple. If you want to know more about using charts I can thoroughly recommend Gene Zelazny's booklet *Choosing and Using Charts* published by Video Arts Ltd.

155

Summary

1 *Check the layout:*

- spacing

- margins

- headings

- sections

- paragraphs

- lists

2 *Use appendices*

3 *Charts and graphs:*

- for component comparison use pie charts

- for item comparison use bar charts

- for time series comparison use column charts or line charts

- for frequency distribution use column charts

- for correlation use bar charts or dot charts.

4 *Flow charts*

- work-flow charts: to show how people or work moves around a location

- schematic flow charts: for an overview of the stages of a process or project

- detailed flow charts: to show how work moves around between functions.

10
■ ■ ■

Topping and tailing

If you're cooking a special meal which you hope will satisfy every-one's hunger and impress them at the same time, you wouldn't dream of serving it up without a garnish. And if you're writing a proposal or report which you hope will satisfy everyone's need for information and impress them at the same time – well, that also needs a garnish.

There are lots of extra bits and pieces – some of them very important – to add to reports and proposals. Some of these are standard and some you may need only occasionally. This is the last chapter – apart from the final review – because everything in this chapter should be written after you've finished the main body of the report or proposal, even if it doesn't eventually go at the back of the report. The function of these parts of the docu-ment is to put the report or proposal in context, and give sup-porting information.

Putting the report or proposal in context
■ ■ ■

If you flick through this book you'll find the sort of thing I mean. This book has a title page, information about publishers and copyright, contents, index, acknowledgements. Other books on other subjects might have a section on further reading, a bibliography, useful addresses or even a glossary. Your report or proposal needs to have the same kind of packaging.

Regular features

I can't swear that every single proposal or report will always have every one of these features – a memo for example, which is a form of short report, probably won't. And you may have a house style which you are obliged to follow. But as a rule you would expect to include these most of the time:

- title page with title and author
- contents page
- the objective (sometimes you have to reword this slightly to make it appropriate for the reader)
- summary (we'll look at that in more detail later)
- appendices
- page numbers.

Other features

From time to time you will probably find these other features helpful for the reader:

- acknowledgements of other people who have helped or contributed

- conclusion page (for longer reports you may also want to provide a brief summary of the conclusions)
- glossary, if you have had to use jargon that your readers may not understand
- bibliography
- references (to the sources you've used)
- further addresses.

References

As always, the more you can boost your credibility the better. So list the sources you used for your report or proposal. Then if anyone is inclined to challenge you on the validity of any of the data you quote, you can show them that it came from a respected source. These sources will be the same ones we looked at in Chapter 2, such as:

- interviews with experts, customers or colleagues
- books (if there are several, or they are important, it would be better to list them in a bibliography)
- catalogues, brochures, annual reports etc.
- internal reports
- media sources – magazines, newspaper articles etc.
- research reports
- trade associations
- local authorities, government departments.

It's also a good idea to give the dates of the research, as some of the data may change during the lifetime of the proposal or report.

The summary

Unless your report is extremely brief, some of your readers may not have time to read it all. Even if they do, they may want to recap it later without having to read the whole thing again. What they need is a summary. Not a summary in the sense of a conclusion, but a précis or résumé which briefly summarises the report or proposal.

Every report or proposal which runs to more than three or four pages should have a summary at the beginning, straight after the contents page. So what should you put in it? If you think about it, it's quite simple. If this is the only part of the report that some of your readers will see, you want to include everything. Only shorter.

The summary should be a miniature version of the report or proposal, complete in itself, so the key facts are clear to anyone who reads it, even if they read nothing else. This being the case, it should obviously follow the same structure as the full version:

- either the four 'P's, or
- Aim, Method, Results, Conclusion.

It should be clear why it is far more sensible to write the summary *after* you've written the main body of the document.

EXERCISE

Write a brief summary for a proposal to your board of directors who want to celebrate ten years in business by taking the whole company on an unusual day trip. They've asked you to come up with three suggestions, and recommend the one you think is best.

RESPONSE

Objective

To examine three good options for day trips for the whole company to celebrate ten years in business; the cost should be under £100 a head and the alternatives should be unusual and exciting.

Position

The company has been in business for ten years and prides itself on a strong and loyal relationship with its employees.

Problem

The tenth anniversary is approaching and the directors would like to find something special to do for the staff. Rather than the usual anniversary drinks party they would like to take everyone for an unusual day out.

Possibilities

The three possibilities under consideration are:

1   A hot air balloon trip.

    This is very popular with some members of staff, but three suffer from vertigo and would prefer not to join in. The actual trip lasts for about two hours. It is quite expensive so there would be very little change left over for, say, providing dinner for everyone at the end of the day.

2   An 'adventure caving' trip.

    Like the hot air balloon, most people would love to do this, but a significant handful would find it so nerve-wracking that they wouldn't want to join the group. The trips last about three hours, and are relatively inexpensive.

3   A boat trip down the river.

    This could last all day, and include a light lunch and dinner within the budget. Only about a quarter of people in the company would put this as their first choice, but everybody would be satisfied with it.

Proposal

The only option to which no-one objects is the day's boat trip on the river, so this seems to be the best idea. Although perhaps not the most exciting option, it is still quite unusual. On an occasion of this sort it seems fairer and more considerate on the part of the directors to do something which doesn't exclude anyone.

163

Summary

Include in your proposal or report:

- title page
- author's name
- contents page
- summary
- appendices
- page numbers.

Consider using the following:

- acknowledgements
- conclusion page
- glossary
- bibliography
- references
- further addresses etc.

11
■ ■ ■
Review

That's it, really. We've looked at all the important lessons of writing reports and proposals. And in the process we've covered a lot of key skills which are vital to other areas of management as well. Once you know how to set an objective, structure, write straightforward English and present material clearly, you automatically understand many of the vital management skills which apply to areas such as:

- selling

- organising exhibitions

- planning presentations

- letter writing

- project planning

- market research

- writing job applications.

This final chapter gives you a chance to practise all the lessons of proposal and report writing together. The chapter is divided into three sections:

1 The first part of the chapter is a proposal for introducing flexible working hours into the company. You shouldn't find it hard to spot the mistakes; the real challenge is to rewrite it using the skills we've covered in this book.

2 In the second section, you'll find a checklist of all the main points to remember when producing proposals and reports. Use this as a reminder as you rewrite the report.

3 Finally, I've included an improved version of the proposal for you to compare with your own. Do remember, though, that no two versions will ever look exactly the same. You just need to make sure that you've followed all the main rules.

The proposal: version 1
■ ■ ■

Here's the first part of the exercise – you shouldn't have much difficulty finding room for improvement. Once you've read it, go through the checklist that follows. Then re-read the report once for each section of the checklist, looking out for the points which are relevant to that section.

PROPOSAL: FLEXIBLE WORKING HOURS

In undertaking an initial study into the potential introduction of flexible working hours into the company there are a number of points to consider. For the most part the employees appear to receive the idea positively although some resist it; however it is probably a good idea to do it in such a way that it is an optional course of action for staff and those that are unreceptive are not obligated to conform to it. A proportion of employees have been approached and consulted already on their attitude to the idea in principal and their response seems to vary according to age-group and gender in particular. Their views are summarised as follows:

AGE GROUP	MEN Total number consulted	MEN Positive response	MEN Negative number response	WOMEN Total	WOMEN positive response	WOMEN Negative response
18–30	20	19	1	18	18	0
30–40	23	19	4	29	29	2
40–50	15	8	7	12	12	4
50–60	12	2	10	8	7	1

There are several different approaches which could be adopted towards the introduction of flexible working. Working hours could be restricted to certain times of day which, although more flexible than at present, could still be limited. For example employees could have the scope to commence work any time between the hours of 8.30 am and 9.30 am and to terminate between 4.30 pm and 5.30 pm. However it should be borne in mind that many of the female employees who favour a more flexible pattern of work do so on account of their commitment to their families especially in terms of the transportation of children to and from their place of education, and for these staff this limited degree of flexibility would be insufficient. On the other hand it would be the least resource-heavy method to implement, and could be developed further towards greater flexibility in future.

Another potential approach would be to install time clocks and for all employees to be instructed to clock on and off whenever they enter or leave the workplace. All contracts would in any case specify the number of hours to be worked for each designated period of time and the clock would indicate when the *employee had reached their* alloted time input. Using this method it would be possible to extend the range of time during which employees could attend the workplace. Parts of the worksite could be available from as early as 7.30 am through until 8.00 pm. Employees could then elect to attend the workplace on certain days only, remaining for sufficiently extended hours to negate the need to attend on other days. This would also carry with it a greater level of convenience for parents who wish to be available for family commitments at specific times, or for any employee with obligations of such a nature outside the workplace, since they could absent themselves from the workplace and return at a later time on the same day. This would apply similarly to employees wishing to absent themselves from the workplace for reasons such as medical appointments. Under the present arrangement these employees are usually given permission to be absent for a period of time without such absence being reflected in their monthly remuneration. Under a flexible working arrangement such time away from the workplace would automatically be deducted from the employee's running total of hours worked. This would be beneficial to the company as time spent away from the workplace would no longer have to be paid for. Many employees, however, would be dispirited at this approach as they feel at present that reasonable time off for such eventualities as medical appointments or serious family crises are a natural and reasonable benefit of the job. To effectively remove these 'perks' would render them unmotivated and would cause them to feel that the company did not deem them trustworthy.

One option that must be considered worthy of consideration is to retain the current situation and reject the proposal for any alteration to it. The present arrangement has been found to be acceptable hitherto and although there is pressure for change this is not so considerable, at least not to date, as to render it unworkable in future. Any alteration to the system will incur complications in its implementation and by the same token the continuation of the present system will negate this potential for problems and increased expenditure. Since the company adopts this system at present it is evident that it is at the least workable.

One of the difficulties that may be incurred by adopting a highly flexible approach is that there is a minimum staffing level required in the workplace during standard, conventional business hours in order for the company to function effectively. In consideration of this it would therefore be necessary to restrict employees' flexibility, or at least that of some employees, to ensure minimum cover in all departments at all times. It is probable that this would lead to different levels of permitted flexibility for different employees, depending on both their function within the organisation and the requirements of colleagues in their own departments or in other departments with which they are required to liaise.

The prevalent attitude among those questioned would appear to support the principle of change to a more flexible working system in regard to hours of work but at this moment in time it is not yet possible to determine exactly which system would be the most effective. There are certain factors to consider as far as employee requirements are concerned and of these the most frequent aspect specified is that of parents, in particular female workers, who wish to be available at times which currently fall within standard working hours for the purpose of transporting children to and from their place of education. Of the respondents to the initial research who fell into the higher age range, those who favoured the more flexible approach were mostly employees with dependent relatives for whom they function as part-time carers, which can place demands on their time between current commencement and termination hours of work.

170

A final consideration is that of employee motivation in terms both of retaining existing staff and recruiting new employees as and when the demand arises. Employees are better motivated in situations in which they feel they have the co-operation of their employers, and research has been conducted which demonstrates the strong correlation between employee motivation and organisational productivity. In this respect, and in order to remain in line with current thinking on approaches to employee relations, especially in the competitive environment of staff recruitment, a more flexible approach might put the organisation in a stronger position in the market place.

Checklist
■ ■ ■

Set an objective

1   Who are you writing the report or proposal for?

2   What will they want to know?

3   What is their level of knowledge?

4   Make the objective as specific as you can, and write it down in one sentence.

5   If someone else has asked you to write the report or proposal, show them the objective before you start work.

Collect the information

Research

1   Start by deciding what information you need. Using the objective as your reference, list the areas you need to cover.

2   For each of these general areas create a list of specific topics to research.

3   Go and find the information you need – use written sources, publicly available information, and talk to people.

4   Add your own notes of any benefits you want to emphasise.

Organise

5   Copy each point (or a note of it) onto a separate piece of paper.

6   Sort these pieces of paper into logical groups.

Plan the structure – proposals

The four 'P's:

1 *Position: where we are now*

- Make sure you're all agreed on what the proposal is about.

- State the position from the reader's point of view.

2 *Problem: why we can't stay here*

- Could be good or bad.

- Persuade the reader that things can't be left as they are.

3 *Possibilities: all the places we could go instead*

- include this section unless the reader will be making a straight yes/no decision.

- discuss the pros and cons of each option, and draw comparisons between them where this is useful.

4 *Proposal: the best direction to choose*

- If you don't have a 'possibilities' section: explain your proposal, answer any objections and supply facts to support your case.

- If you do have a 'possibilities' section: make a choice and justify it.

Plan the structure – reports

Research reports

Structure into four sections:

- ■ Aim
- ■ Method
- ■ Results
- ■ Conclusion

Information only reports

- ■ Present the information in the logical groups you put it into when you collected it together.

- ■ If it is possible, work through these groups in a logical order.

173

Be persuasive

1 *Show them you're on their side*

- ■ Write from the reader's point of view
- ■ Show you understand the real issues
- ■ Be objective

2 *Lead them over to your side*

- ■ Be fair
- ■ Don't pooh-pooh the other possibilities
- ■ Give the reader an excuse to change their mind
- ■ Put your preferred option last
- ■ Anticipate objections

Use plain English

Style

1 *General approach*

- Match the style to the reader

- Use everyday English

- Be politically correct

- Explain new ideas clearly

2 *Phrasing and sentences*

- Avoid jargon

- Keep away from stock phrases

- Avoid clichés

- Keep sentences and paragraphs short

3 *Words*

- Use short words

- Avoid legal words and pomposity

- Avoid neutral words

- Beware ambiguous words

- Avoid tautology and redundant words

- Use concrete not abstract nouns

- Use active not passive verbs

Mechanics

Check:

- Your choice of words
- Spelling
- Abbreviations

Punctuation:

- Capital letters
- Apostrophes
- Commas
- Colons
- Semi-colons

175

Make it look readable

1 *Check the layout:*

- Spacing
- Margins
- Headings
- Sections
- Paragraphs
- Lists

2 *Use appendices*

3 *Charts and graphs:*

- For component comparison use pie charts

- For item comparison use bar charts

- For time series comparison use column charts or line charts

- For frequency distribution use column charts

- For correlation use bar charts or dot charts.

4 *Flow charts:*

- Work-flow charts: to show how people or work moves around a location

- Schematic flow charts: for an overview of the stages of a process or project

- Detailed flow charts: to show how work moves around between functions.

Top and tail

Include in your proposal or report:

- Title page with title and author

- Contents page

- Summary

- Appendices

- Page numbers.

Consider using the following:

- Acknowledgements

- Conclusion page

- Glossary

- Bibliography

- References

- Further addresses etc.

The proposal: version 2
■ ■ ■

On the next page is an improved version of the proposal. Go through it and compare it with yours; don't expect it to be identical but make sure that the key areas, such as structure, layout and use of English, are similar.

FLEXIBLE WORKING HOURS

An initial study for ABC Ltd.

by

Jane Smith

FLEXIBLE WORKING HOURS

An initial study

Objective

To identify the factors involved in introducing flexible working hours, to examine their benefits and disadvantages and to recommend the best approach to take.

Summary

At present, almost all employees of ABC Ltd work from 9.00 to 5.00. A handful work from 9.30 to 5.30.

Many, though not all, staff are unhappy with this and would prefer a more flexible arrangement. Some are working mothers and would like to be able to collect their children *to and from* school. Some, particularly the older employees, have sick or elderly relatives who make demands on their time which do not fit comfortably with their working hours.

For the company itself, this dissatisfaction among staff leads to low morale and reduced productivity. It also makes it harder to attract and retain good staff.

There are three basic options for the future:

1 *Leave things as they are.* This is obviously less demanding on resources than implementing a new system. At least we know it works even if it isn't perfect.

2 *Highly flexible system.* Employees would clock on and clock off anytime within a $12\frac{1}{2}$ hour working day until they have 'clocked up' 35 hours a week. This would be the hardest system to implement.

3 *Limited flexibility.* Staff could start work any time between 8.00 am to 10.00 am and work through for eight hours. This would not solve all employees' problems but it would solve most of them.

Proposal

Introduce a system of limited flexibility for now, retaining the option of increasing flexibility later if this seems appropriate.

Position

The current working hours at ABC Ltd are 9.00 to 5.00 for most employees, with a few working from 9.30 to 5.30.

Problem

Although this works up to a point, it does have certain disadvantages, both for the organisation and for some of the employees.

The organisation: The chief disadvantage of the current system is that many of the staff are dissatisfied with it. This has become such a serious problem that it is becoming harder to attract and retain good staff. Those staff who do join the company and stay with it feel less motivated: this, as research has shown, means they are less productive than they could be.

The employees: Some employees are satisfied with their current working hours, but many of them find the present system restrictive. There are several reasons for this but the employees most strongly in favour of greater flexibility are, in particular:

- parents, especially mothers, who would prefer to be able to take

  their children to and from school, and to work around this commitment.

- employees, many of them in the older age range, who have elderly or sick relatives who they would like to be more available for.

A more flexible approach would make it easier for many staff to fulfil these kinds of demands on their time.

An initial study questioned nearly 140 employees in a cross-section of ages. A large majority were in favour of a more flexible approach, in particular the women and the younger members of the company. It is worth noting that a minority of staff were against the introduction of flexible working hours. Appendix I gives the full results of this study.

Possibilities

Since this report is looking at the principle and not the detail of a more flexible approach, the options available fall broadly into three categories: retaining the present system, introducing limited flexibility of working hours, and implementing a highly flexible system.

Retaining the present system: I have already outlined above the problem with leaving things as they are. On the plus side however there are one or two points to make.

Although the system is not perfect, at least we know it works. The staff all signed their contracts on the understanding that the company worked to standard hours of business, and while it may not be ideal for them it is at least manageable. Better the devil you know.

Implementing any new system is bound to incur problems and expense, consequently retaining the present working hours is the least expensive option in terms of direct cost.

Highly flexible system: A highly flexible system would mean keeping the site open from, say, 7.30 am to 8.00 pm. All staff are contracted to work a certain number of hours a week and time clocks are installed. Employees simply clock on and off whenever they enter or leave the building, until they have reached their full number of hours each week.

This system has the obvious benefit that it can accommodate a huge degree of flexibility which should suit the various demands of all employees. They could even elect to work 35 hours a week spread over only three days. A further benefit to the company would be that doctors' appointments and so on would no longer happen 'on company time' as they do at present. This system does have several disadvantages, however:

- Many staff regard occasional time off for such things as doctors' appointments or serious family crises as a natural 'perk' of the job. With this system they would have to make up the hours elsewhere. Not only would they lose the time off, but many would also feel that the company did not trust them. This would obviously be bad for company morale.

- It would be difficult to implement this system fairly. The sales office, for example, must be staffed at least from 9.00 to 5.30 every day. What if all the sales staff want to take Friday off? How do you decide who can and who can't? What if the computer goes down at 4 o'clock in the afternoon and there are no computer staff in until 7.30 the following morning?

183

Limited flexibility: This would mean asking employees to continue to work an eight hour day, but give them a range of, say, ten hours to fit it into. They could start any time between 8.00 and 10.00 in the morning, so they would finish eight hours later – between 4.00 and 6.00.

On the plus side, this would give the employees the co-operation and recognition of their problems that many of them look for, and would therefore increase staff motivation. For some it would provide a way around their other commitments.

On the other hand, this approach still does not allow enough flexibility for some of the working mothers, in particular, who want to be available for their children at both ends of the day.

Proposal

Given the number of staff in favour of more flexible working hours, and the importance of staff motivation, it seems sensible to adopt some kind of flexible approach. But it is probably advisable to find a system that allows the significant minority who prefer to stay as they are to do so.

So which is the best system to choose? It is harder to go backwards than forwards in developing new systems: if the highly flexible approach failed it would be difficult to pull back to a less flexible system (in terms of keeping the staff happy). On the other hand, a limited degree of flexibility could easily be extended later if this seemed appropriate.

So at this stage it seems that the most workable system, which contains most of the benefits required by the employees, is the limited flexibility of working hours.

Appendix I

Table of employee responses to the proposal for flexible working hours

AGE GROUP	MEN Total number consulted	MEN Positive response	MEN Negative response	WOMEN Total number consulted	WOMEN positive response	WOMEN Negative response
18–30	20	19	1	18	18	0
30–40	23	19	4	29	27	2
40–50	15	8	7	12	8	4
50–60	12	2	10	8	7	1
	70	48	22	67	60	7

Conclusion

■ ■ ■

So that's it. You should now be able to turn out impressive reports and proposals that get the results you want. And the more you practise the easier you'll find it and the quicker you'll be able to do it. There are just four more points to make:

1 Of course you want to go through your report or proposal and tidy up anything you feel could be improved. But remember to consider the overall potential value of the document and balance it against the value of the time you spend on it. Don't fall into the habit of wasting hours and days tweaking little details that no-one but you would notice.

2 Get someone else to read your proposal or report through before you submit it. No-one is meant to be able to spot everything for themselves. Find someone who is good at spotting spelling mistakes and typographical errors, and who knows and understands the subject about as well as your readers.

3 You've already laid out the document to look clean and smart. Before you submit it, put it in some kind of plastic folder or binder. The more you treat it with respect, the more the readers will.

4 Deliver it on time, without fail.

Of course, these skills should help you in selling, making presentations, negotiating, project planning, research and all the rest of it – and writing books. My objective for this book was: 'To explain in a clear and entertaining way all the skills that are needed, from planning through to delivery, to write reports and proposals that get results.' I hope you feel I've achieved it.

Index

■　■　■

the Institute
of Management
F O U N D A T I O N
PITMAN
PUBLISHING

The Institute of Management/Pitman Publishing *Management Solution Series* provides you with all the know how you need every day of your working life. These books represent the core business skills. Not only will they help you day to day but, if you read the whole series, you will have an impressive skills portfolio to help you gallop up the career ladder.

the Institute
of Management

FOUNDATION

PITMAN
PUBLISHING

The Institute of Management's mission is to promote the development, exercise and recognition of professional management. The Institute's members include all levels of management from students to chief executives. The Institute of Management supports its own Foundation, which provides a unique range of services designed to develop, inform and advise managers in every sector of business.

What has been said about Pitman Publishing/Institute of Management Books:

"Practical guidance on a wide range of management issues"
— *The Independent on Sunday*

"They meet the need for managers to learn fast and to solve problems quickly"
— *Professional Manager*

"These books are presented in a crisp, approachable format and offer practical guidance ... The principles articulated in these books are important"
— *The Independent*

"Written in an accessible and jargon free style. Packed with helpful advice tips and tricks"
— *Business North West*

"For busy managers with little time for training, these quick to follow guides will help develop the skills to ensure they are the best in the business"
— *Jeremy Kourdi, Institure of Management*

"Certain to become a lifeline for managers"
— *Commerce Magazine*